C0-AKB-632

Praise for *The Comforter:*

"A beautiful book. Teresa is a storyteller, a quilt-weaver, a woman who has found her voice — a woman of faith. This book will weave the patches of your life into a quilt of *real,* not pious, faith."

—Paul Morrissey, O.S.A., Author of *Let Someone Hold You,*
Winner, 1995 Christopher Award

"A tenderly evocative and compelling contribution to narrative theology, to women's spirituality, and to a newly evolving Catholic, religious sensibility which dares to hear the global cries of the poor."

—Janet Ruffing, R.S.M., Ph.D., Spirituality and
Spiritual Direction, Fordham University

"Teresa Rhodes McGee's stories point to the core of humanity, where crusts have melted away and our yearning mingles with God's, who weeps for us with unquenchable love."

—Barbara Fiand, S.N.D.deN., Author of *Wrestling with God*
and *Embraced by Compassion*

"These are stories of such faith and hope, such love and suffering,... that they reveal the deepest parts of who we are, even as they reveal a God of Presence and Compassion."

—John Shea, Co-author of *Fires of Desire*

"Drenched with the Presence of God. There *is* Light at the end of the tunnel! An amazing book."

—Nancy Benvenga, Ph.D., Author of
Healing the Pain of Emotional Abuse

To my precious
Sister — Mary Jane —

The
Comforter

May you find the
peace of the Comforter
in the quiet moments
of your life.
Love Always
Eileen

The Comforter

Stories of Loss and Rebirth

TERESA RHODES MCGEE

A Crossroad Book
The Crossroad Publishing Company
New York

1997

The Crossroad Publishing Company
370 Lexington Avenue, New York, NY 10017

Copyright © 1997 by Teresa Rhodes McGee

All rights reserved. No part of this book may be reproduced, stored in a retrieval system, or transmitted, in any form or by any means, electronic, mechanical, photocopying, recording, or otherwise, without the written permission of The Crossroad Publishing Company.

Printed in the United States of America

Library of Congress Cataloging-in-Publication Data

McGee, Teresa Rhodes.
    The comforter : stories of loss and rebirth / Teresa Rhodes McGee.
      p.   cm.
    ISBN 0-8245-1567-6 (pbk.)
      1. Suffering — Religious aspects — Christianity. 2. Consolation.
3. Christian life.   I. Title.
BV4909.M345   1997
248.8'6–dc20   97–12528

Contents

Acknowledgments

This book came into being through the faith of many people who blessed my life with their confidence, encouragement, and support. First among those believers is my husband, Dick, whose care, support, humor, and vision are joyful gifts that make it possible not only to write but to live. Our sons, Michael and Patrick, call me to laugh, teach me to see the world in new and wonderful ways, and keep me grounded in the basic realities of life.

The genesis of *The Comforter* was a three-page essay assigned by Dr. Janet Ruffing, RSM, at Fordham University. I am most grateful for her encouragement to develop the work and for the help of Dr. John Shea, OSA, also of Fordham, who read it in an intermediate stage and made good on his promise to bug me until I published. Without their support and encouragement I would never have had the courage to continue my work. I am indebted to Lynn Schmitt Quinn, who served as both editor and midwife for this project.

Several people made the actual process of writing possible. I especially thank Susan Weissert and Larry Rich, Betty and Frank Maurovich, Rita Reichert, Kathy McAleer, Scott Harris, Larry Lewis, Vinnie and Denise Bilotta, and Gary Hellman for the gracious, treasured ways in which each lent breath to my voice. Finally, I thank my family and friends, whose love through the years has taught me that life, like a patchwork quilt, is of one blessed piece.

INTRODUCTION

The Comforter

❧

And I will pray the Father,
and he shall give you another Comforter. . . .
I will not leave you comfortless.

—John 14:16, 18

I AM NOT by talent or disposition given to needlework. Thus it came as something of a surprise to me that when I discovered my paternal grandmother's quilt pieces in a closet, I felt compelled to complete her project. As I spread the pieces of cloth on the floor to plan my work, I was deeply touched by them; they connected me to the shadows of Grandma's life and the promising youth in which she had cast tiny stitches and formed patterns of beauty. Much of Grandma's life was filled with betrayal and wrapped in a silence that hid the wounds of her illusory world. The memory of my grandmother's life, including her lost creativity and her suffering, was folded into the unfinished pattern. To complete the quilt felt like a necessary act of love.

When I went to the library to search for quilting instructions, I found a yellowed book on the history of quilting that helped me to understand the symbolic power of my grandmother's quilt pieces. While quilting has ancient roots, patchwork quilts have their origin in an act of resistance to the British colonial cloth embargo. Patching together their rags and binding them to any available materials, the colonists made quilts that protected them from the cold and enabled them to resist the economic and political pressures of the British embargo. The patchwork quilts allowed the colonists to survive in an incomprehensible and uncontrollable wilderness. From those origins, an art form developed. Over time patchwork quilting evolved into a process in which American women took their scraps of cloth and, following an ancient ritual of women expressing in textiles what can't be said in words, made comforter patterns that told their stories.

With quilting as an ongoing part of life, no scrap of cloth was insignificant, no garment ever discarded. Even the smallest piece of fabric could become part of a new design.

The cycle of the year set the rhythm for quilting; through the lonely, isolating winters, individual women made their unique squares and patterns. The summer brought women together for the communal activity of joining the squares and layers of one another's quilts in preparation for the next winter. Women expressed their memories, hopes, and yearnings through their patchwork designs, through the patterns of their quilting stitches, and by tucking ragged edges under in a transformative testimony of their lives. The design was carefully backed with a harmonious cloth that held together the new and the old without tearing apart the gathered remnants.

Quilting provided women with a means of creatively breaking the silence about their experiences. Patterns emerged that reflected history, geography, personal experience, and, at times, forbidden political opinions. Before universal suffrage, it was not uncommon for women to cast their vote on the marriage bed by stitching the symbols of their preferred political party into the quilt, often unknown to husbands who held conflicting political views. During the years of the underground railroad, the quilt hanging on the clothesline in a certain way was a sign that exodus was possible that very night.

The power of the quilt as a symbol is its invitation to make meaning in life by letting the tattered scraps of our experiences and our doubt be the raw materials of a new creation. Through the centuries, spiritual masters have written that the most profound invitation to encountering God comes in the experience of suffering, death, and limitation. St. John of the Cross wrote that transformation of the soul happens when the limits of understanding are embraced and we allow ourselves to be remade in the darkness of God's seeming failure to protect us from suffering.

Pain is always an invitation to enter the heart of the paschal mystery. Our experience of pain brings us into close relationship and communion with Jesus' suffering, death, and resurrection and challenges all our assumptions about control. This is a very different approach to human suffering than the prevailing cultural view that pain is a negative experience to be managed and thus rendered invisible. It is quite different from my own proclivity to make meaning by constructing an intellectual order that leaves no room for mystery or unanswered questions. Indeed, pain is one of the truths of experience — fidelity to it helps lead us to encounter and understand the whole of life.

We tend the pieces of our truths by letting the stories of life be told, believing that in each person's narrative, God is revealed. We all long to find comfort by making a quilt of these truths. When we allow God to be the harmonious cloth that holds our stories and symbols, the experience of pain is transformative in its power to connect us to the deeper truths of love and to one another.

Much as I would want it to be otherwise, the truth of life is that people are deeply hurt; the innocent suffer and die; and the world is filled with violence, oppression, and poverty. Yet equally true is the human capacity to retain hope, to give expression to a vision of a better life, and to create community by stitching our sorrows, joys, and commitments into one cloth. That capacity is born of God, and it brings us a wholeness that makes resistance to evil and oppression possible.

This book is a quilt, a comforter born of resistance. I've gathered stories of seemingly meaningless, unconnected suffering and have connected them to one another and to God. Through these connections, the tyranny of the suffering they describe is transformed. The pieces of my quilt are made from scraps of memory-making symbols, pieces of bread that became communion, unexpected hope that engendered courage, and faith that nourished love in the daily round. Each reflection, like a square in a quilt, has its own unity, its own limitation, and its own ragged edges of doubt. The stories are made from fabric that I worked with in stages and pieces; by surprise and against my conscious will, they came to warm, comfort, and nurture my soul. Each piece of the quilt tells of life's blessings being discovered not in the experience of being filled but in the emptying of the heart described in the Beatitudes.

The stories are deeply personal, as they must be if they are to bear witness to the truth of the heart's transformation. Their personal quality makes them part of a larger quilt; the remnants of memory and experience from any life have common threads that easily connect them to a larger human story and God's harmonious cloth. The stories, spanning a range of time and geography, are stitched together with the strong thread of our common biblical story and are, as such, an expression of gratitude for the sustaining presence of God.

There has been unexpected comfort in my connecting the stories, as if the prayerful, winter solitude in which they were written was intended to teach me that my memories, dreams, doubts, and longings are meant to be woven into our shared faith story. I offer this quilt to others in the hope that it will both create warmth and bear witness to the wonder of our grandmothers' stitches: the fabric of faith that holds the memory of suffering and rebirth is stronger than time and death. Our calling is to reverence the pieces, to connect them, and to be made holy in the comforting awareness of God's presence and love.

CHAPTER ONE

Communion of Saints

*We are for our part surrounded
by this cloud of witnesses.*

—HEBREWS 12:1

L ARRY WALKS GINGERLY on toes with circulation compromised by diabetes. He is a tall man and gentle by nature; even before the troubles in his toes led him to wear special shoes, Larry walked with deliberate care. Neither a clashing gong nor a booming cymbal, his gait is that of a man who has found his dignity from within and, knowing what matters most in life, is unafraid to stop and be attentive to the people around him. Larry's attentiveness forms a faith-filled bridge between people who probably would not otherwise meet and who certainly would not have the same appreciation for each other without his inviting presence. Quietly, gently, and slowly, Larry leads people to think about the needs of the world around them and to respond to that world out of commitment to the future.

Larry was the youngest deacon in the history of Mount Olivet Baptist Church in Peekskill, New York. He possessed a wisdom that led all of the other church officers to respect and listen to him. Larry was quiet, never conspicuous; however, his sound thinking, goal-centeredness, and faithful presence made him a strong leader.

As a single man, he purchased a home that he cared for meticulously. It was to that home that he brought Eva after their marriage. Eva brought a steady presence to Larry's life, loving him gently and supporting his work. She was different from Larry in ways that were complementary and fulfilling. For them God was too important to be confined to a building or a specific space; anchored in their church, their belief in God carried over into all aspects of life. In the different ways of their personalities,

Larry and Eva set out to build a foundation for future generations, committed, as Larry would say, "to leaving something for
our children." Larry's and Eva's sense of home was expansive:
they took in several foster children, including two young boys
they raised. Larry and Eva believed in these children when no
one else did, and by doing so they inspired and encouraged many
other people.

Larry, who had limited opportunities for education himself,
worked to develop a tutoring and scholarship program within the
church. If Larry was aware of a difficulty in the local school,
he might begin by talking with the teacher or local princi-
pal. If need be, he might quietly go to see the superintendent
of schools, insisting on a quality of education that would help
children aspire toward excellence. He formed partnerships with
people whose formal education far surpassed his own. No one
ever thought to ask Larry about his qualifications for speaking
to or addressing a particular problem or issue; he simply never
allowed an opportunity for doubt. Larry's heart did not seem to
have a place in it for jealousy or competition; there was too much
to be done, too many problems to address, too many people
needing encouragement.

In the 1960s, Larry went to work as a custodian at a Catholic
seminary, a job he has held through three decades and untold
changes in his life and in the world. There he met young men
studying to be missionary priests and many lay men and women
who were involved in the missionary enterprise and who passed
through his life for a short period of time. Larry believed that
anyone who was to be a good Catholic minister of Christ needed
to have a positive experience of an African-American Protestant
church. So, quietly and without long theories about ecumenism,
Larry began a ministry of invitation. He invited people — one-
by-one and two-by-two — to come and worship in his church.

Through times of social upheaval and explosive race relations, Larry brought people of diverse backgrounds together by inviting them all to sing praises to God.

He always had time to listen to people, and he remembered over distance and years the details of people's lives, their stories and aspirations. He was a steady presence welcoming home missioners whose spirits were tired from the suffering and limitations they had experienced, and he challenged all he met to be faithful in their daily lives. Wherever he was, Larry offered encouragement to people, recognizing in his church both the students who excelled and those who had no one to encourage them. He invited the head of a Catholic order and the broken man he met on the street to come to the church and feel at home in the presence of the community and the one God.

And wherever Larry was, Eva offered him encouragement. Her spirit was a well of strength from which Larry drew. Eva had a calming effect on Larry and helped him weather the impatience he felt in the midst of so much that needed to be done to improve life for the people around him. They worked together to make their home a place of harmony and invitation. They lived hospitably, befriending dozens of people over the years. Their compassionate hearts made the stranger welcome in their home, their church, and their community. Larry and Eva gave people what they needed for their bodies (food, bedding, and clothing) and what they needed for their souls (friendship, faith, and hope). They knew too well the effects of racism and hatred. They daily experienced the prejudice in American society, sometimes subtle, sometimes overt, but certainly ever present. They met that prejudice, and the hatred that fueled it, with dignity, courage, and, perhaps most significantly, a love that embodied their desire to make the world a better place for all, especially children.

They lived their faith together for more than thirty years of ordinary days that together formed better or worse, richer or poorer, sickness and health, a promise to be together forever. It was on one such ordinary day that Eva walked out of the house to go to work and never returned. Larry would later say that the only thing unusual about Eva that day was that she looked exceptionally beautiful. "I almost said something to her," Larry said, "because she just looked so pretty and alive that day. It was like she floated. I almost asked her if she was doing something special that day because she looked so fine." However, time for comments about beauty had quickly gotten away from him. It was going to be a hot day, and they both wanted to leave early for their jobs. Their conversation turned to what to have for supper. Eva said she would make chicken when she got home; Larry said that whatever she made would be fine. Eva said good-bye to Larry, walked past her carefully tended flower garden, and, looking very beautiful, drove away from their impeccable brick house.

Larry received the phone call a few hours later. Eva had fainted at work and been taken to the hospital. Larry was told to come as quickly as possible. By the time he arrived, it was clear that Eva had suffered a massive stroke and was in critical condition. Larry called his sons and the pastor whom, years earlier, he had identified as a spiritual leader. Together they made the decision to allow a surgical procedure to reduce the pressure on Eva's brain. What followed was a week-long vigil in which it was clear, from the beginning, that Eva had entered the passageway of death. She never regained consciousness. Eva had always been physically strong; she had delivered her babies without difficulty, had been very energetic all of her life, and had cared for Larry when he had had health problems. No one expected that life and death would turn the tables on assumptions and expectations, making it Larry who stood in the intensive care unit praying for a miracle. Eva's vitality gave the vigil an element of unreality; this was clearly some terrible mistake. Further, it seemed impossible that she could be silenced so quickly on a day when she had looked so alive.

The compassion with which Larry and Eva had lived was measured back to them in the agony of Eva's illness and death. Given the nature of their lives, it was not surprising that so many people came to stand with Larry and his sons in an outpouring of concern, gratitude, and love expressed in words and simple actions. People waited with them, cleaned their house, prepared food. Throughout Eva's last days, Larry talked about her the way he always had, with reverence, respect, and a deep love. He talked with admiration about her patience and her dedication. There were also moments when Larry's silence expressed his pain and exhaustion. While he had no doubt that Eva was going to a better place, her struggles and sorrows to be received by a God who would raise her to new life, the vigil of her death was wrenching. Each day that Eva lay dying deepened Larry's pain, and the prayers of those who loved both of them quickly became pleas for Eva's repose to come quickly. She died quietly on a beautiful summer day.

Her wake was held on a Sunday evening at Mount Olivet Church. A wide cross-section of people came to the church to mourn Eva and bring comfort to Larry and his family. The gracious hospitality with which visitors had always been received at the church deepened at Eva's wake. Larry made a point of introducing each of us to his family, the pastor of the church, and the people who stood prayerfully by Eva's coffin. He invited one of the priests to sit with the family and lead some of the prayers. Beckoned by the commonality of our love and care for Larry's family, black and white, Baptist and Catholic, family and guests, we kept vigil in the church. Eva's body and her spirit were in the center of our vision, creating a profound communion of broken hearts. Clearly Eva's presence on earth would be missed.

All who came to worship at the funeral the next day were warmly welcomed. The pastor took particular care to include everyone gathered in the prayers and singing, inviting us all to be united in the love of God. Many details of Eva's life were filled in during the funeral. The pastor spoke eloquently about her work in the church, saying that her spirit touched and benefited everyone she met. He spoke of her patient teaching of children in an after-school program. He spoke about her gentle mothering of her own two sons and the two foster sons raised by Eva and Larry. He spoke of her care for all who were around her and her steadfast spirit. He described a courage drawn from faith that informed her in all of life's difficulties and joys.

As the pastor named each of Eva's gifts, people in the church shook their heads in agreement and said to each other, "That's right." The telling of Eva's story made her gracious spirit present in the church, a presence that engendered gratitude and hope in the midst of sadness. The pastor concluded the sermon by saying, "Eva lived a faithful, beautiful life, and now she has gone home." Trusting that Eva was indeed home, we prayed, sang, and praised the God that Eva loved. Then we formed a funeral procession, and after passing by Larry and Eva's house, we took her body to the cemetery and gave her back to God.

Larry returned to work a few days later, carefully and slowly going about the activities that structured his life. It happened that those were times of great institutional tension in the place where Larry and I worked — changes that sometimes caused us to be short with one another or, more destructively, draw lines of separation. We were united, however, in the pain of a gentle man whose loss broke through that tension and reminded us to be more faithful and loving in daily life. Our concern for Larry gave us an opportunity to draw from the better part of ourselves; somehow our daily frustrations were less important than his suffering. As he had done so often, Larry caused us to be more attentive, to pause and reflect on Eva's fidelity, and to be more conscious of our importance in one another's lives. Though Larry was devastated by grief, he kept open a window in his soul that allowed a certain grace to shine forth from him and enter each of our lives as he invited us to be with him.

A week after Eva's funeral, I received a phone call that my Uncle John had died in Iowa. John had suffered from several life-threatening conditions, including severe pneumonia, which had necessitated his being placed on a respirator. My cousins had endured a terrible vigil in the intensive care unit, powerlessness in the face of the likely outcome deepening with each passing week, each new medical procedure, and the curse of John's being conscious of his dying. This was not a man who surrendered easily. During World War II, John was a fighter pilot. At the height of the war in the Pacific, he sank an enemy ship after he had been fired upon, a series of events that led John to bob in a life raft in very deep waters and to receive the Navy Cross for heroism. John later married my mother's sister Alice, whose vitality and humor were extraordinary. Together they had nine children, one of whom died in infancy. John and Alice gifted their children with strength, humor, intelligence, and courage. Like Larry, John bore a series of sorrows and losses, including Alice's vitality being suddenly overcome by a fatal cancer. As John aged, the grief he carried more and more appeared to be congenital, as if its deep roots held the losses of several lifetimes. John received daily Communion in the church where he had been baptized, his prayers and worldview held in the experience and symbols of Roman Catholicism. That faith sustained him in ways that gave him energy for living, and, like Larry and Eva, his belief in God spilled over into all aspects of life.

As I flew to Iowa for Uncle John's funeral, an expression of sympathy offered by Larry echoed in my heart. Speaking from his grief to mine, Larry told me that he would pray for my family. And I knew that he would offer those prayers from a heart torn by fresh sorrow. During the flight I thought about heroism and the meaning of a "faithful, beautiful life." I felt strangely accompanied in my journey as if Larry's promise of prayer opened my eyes to the heroism both Eva and John expressed in the course of their day-to-day lives: they loved; they worked; and with inviting, hospitable spirits, they gave themselves to others with a beautiful fidelity that clearly did not end with death.

When I arrived in Iowa, I knew which way to turn on some roads I hadn't driven for a decade, their landmarks etched in a trustworthy place inside me that held patterns and landscape in a living order. There was nothing unknown in the order of the wake service, and it seemed that no one needed introduction. A woman I had never met walked up to me and said, "I told my husband when you walked in the room, 'She's got to be one of the Kennedys.' Whose daughter are you?" I should not have been surprised by her recognition because the Kennedy cousins look so much alike that we joke about having interchangeable parts. Having lived most of my adult life away from Iowa, however, it was unusual to have a stranger correctly place me within my own context, using the family name that had never been part of my own.

It was from those comforting, physical roots that we prayed and sang at John's funeral. We were in the church where John had daily prayed, where the cousins had been baptized and married, where we'd stood over time and waited while the priest blessed the bodies of Grandma and Grandpa Kennedy, Alice, Uncle Jim, and many others. It was somehow the most deeply familiar of all of the familiar places. The words of the liturgy flowed forward as naturally as one's own breath; there was no need for the pastor to give much information about the service because everyone in the church had been there before dozens of times. The church was filled with people who had been touched by John and other members of the family. Two pews were full of postal workers, men and women who had worked with John: their presence was a tribute to him and another reminder of fidelity lived in small actions. The men and women sacrificed the coolest part of the August day to attend the funeral, knowing that they would have to finish their routes in the heat of the afternoon. Each of them, in their fidelity to a friend, brought a certain beauty to the service.

After the funeral we made our way to the section of the cemetery that, in a rather unforgiving understanding of hallowed ground, was designated for Catholics. Having so recently attended Eva's burial, I was struck by the division of the cemetery; it seemed strange to draw lines in so common an experience as death and grief. The priest drew us back to universalities as he read from the burial rite that "Christ, by the three days he spent in the tomb, made the grave a holy place." It was a most comforting idea. We left John's body in that holiness shared by all graves. He was buried next to those whose deaths still were fresh wounds and ancestors who had courageously crossed the sea and given us, into the third generation, identifiable memories, dreams, and faces from Ireland. Driving out of the cemetery, I felt their spirits and memories as much a part of me as the physical characteristics I had inherited from them, a presence that was as comforting as God's presence in the experience of death.

And I felt that Eva was also there, in a faithful place that transcends both sin and death: a spiritual place where we all are one in the death and resurrection of Christ.

Early the next morning, I flew from the familiar place of the ancestors to the anonymity of New York City, enveloped in a presence of home deeper than one life or its geography. I felt myself to be in the presence of the cloud of witnesses described in Scripture, a cloud composed of faces I recognized. Twice in the course of a week I had celebrated the powerful experience of how one life touches another, and in the process, I had become a bit more grounded and trusting in a continuity between heaven and earth. Feeling accompanied by people whose lives were holy and ordinary, I found myself comforted by a familiar understanding of life in which I knew where, and how, to turn.

When I went back to work, the first person I saw was Larry. He again offered his sympathy and asked me about John's funeral. We then talked a bit about Eva's funeral, and I told him again how welcomed I had felt in his church. "You need to be with your people during these times," he said. "All the people who care need to come together. You all came together for my wife's funeral, and that lifted the burden." When I asked how he was feeling, he replied, "Oh, I get along. There are lots of people to help me, but every day it is still so strange." He talked about the suddenness of Eva's death, commenting again that "she looked beautiful the day I married her, and she looked beautiful the day she walked out the door and passed." We both stood silently for a moment in the sacred space of common grief.

The following Saturday my sons, husband, and I went to Larry's house for dinner. He showed us around the house, carefully describing the different things that Eva had done, making her present as he spoke. Larry taught my sons how to talk to Eva's bird, saying as he did so, "The bird knows that everything has changed." After we had eaten Larry's huge and delicious dinner, he walked us around the garden, showing us which flowers had been tended by Eva. We sat outside as the shadows of the evening gave way to dusk. We were all aware of the empty space created by Eva's death. There was in Larry that night the same quiet faith and the same constitutional grief that I associated with John. I perceived as well the faith that would carry Larry through the deepest of pain. Larry sent us home with bowls of leftovers and a heartfelt invitation to come again. He stood on the porch until we had backed out of the driveway; then he turned and entered his quiet house alone.

While we were driving home, I thought of John and Eva. On some levels, their lives could not have been more different — she, an African-American woman living in New York State; he, an Irish-American who had lived most of his days in a small town in Iowa. Their funerals were, by the same measures, vastly different: one held at Mount Olivet Baptist Church, one at the Church of St. Thomas Aquinas, with different rhythms to different songs, all of them sung to the one God. There was a profound humanity in their lives that carried over in the way death transformed them. Eva and John were both people of faith who bore daily witness to their faith by overcoming obstacles and pain. They were people whose presence in the world brought comfort and strength, their hearts holding hope strong enough to be transmitted to the new generation. Both of them uniquely bridged barriers of race, creed, and circumstance as they shared their hearts and homes. In death it was heaven and earth they bridged, their spirits bringing us mortals into the very heart of God. Eva's funeral, with its grief, hospitality, and hope, had given me a broad context in which to experience a sense of belonging. John's funeral, with its familiar faces, ritual, and prayers, gave me a deep sense of rootedness and belonging to a particular family. Both lives bore witness to the truth that relationships transcend even the boundaries of life and death.

In a mysterious way, Larry's life and faith created the bridge to experience different lives and realities as one in God's calling to make our earth a hospitable home. Revealed in the living and the remembering, the communion of saints crosses boundaries, expands identity, and gives strength to believe that those whose stories we carry stay with us. At no point is that sense of communion more powerful than when we walk together into the heart of what we don't understand, from premature death to cursed consciousness. It is then that we know the saints are beautifully and faithfully alive in the paradox of ordinary days that become, through their presence, the hospitable sanctuary of everlasting life.

CHAPTER TWO

Carol's Charities

But she gave from her want,
all that she had to live on.

—MARK 13:44

Her name was Carol, and I knew her only from a distance. My friend's aunt by marriage, she and I crossed paths occasionally through church-related activities. She was a tall woman with hair dyed bright red for as long as anyone could remember. Her hair created a striking contrast with the worn look on her face and her quiet ways. People wondered aloud, sometimes, why she chose that particular color.

Most of what I learned about Carol came from my friend and from considerable speculation around several kitchen tables about why, at the age of sixty-five, Carol had taken a job cleaning tables at McDonald's. No one could understand why she worked. Money was not an issue. Her husband owned a successful hardware store, and everybody knew that he had inherited a chunk of land upstate that had sold for a handsome amount. Why would Carol work at McDonald's? She greeted people she knew when they came into the restaurant but offered no words about her work. She quietly went about her chores, with the care and consistency she showed in her own kitchen. Everyone agreed that she did a good job; it just didn't seem to make sense. And sometimes there were a few whispers that she might not quite be in her right mind.

My friend heard through the family grapevine that Carol's job made her husband furious, in large part because he couldn't figure it out either. When someone asked him at a family gathering if the nail business had taken a turn for the worse, Carol's husband tartly replied, "I have no damn idea why she works there or what she does with the money." The cousin who had posed the question quickly backed off, recognizing that he had hit a nerve and was running the risk of arousing a rather notorious temper.

People had always known about Carol's husband's temper, though no one called it by its proper name. He was given to rage over insignificant things, and though there had been whispers over the years about physical abuse, neither Carol nor her children confided family secrets, and, according to my friend, no relatives of the family pressed to learn things they didn't want to know. Carol worked in the hardware store most of her life in addition to raising her five children. The youngest child was born with Down's syndrome and its accompanying heart defect, something Carol's husband always said must have come from her side of the family. For the four years the little girl lived, Carol cared for her with a tenderness that was part of the town's collective memory, as was the silence with which she grieved the child's death. Until she began her various jobs outside the home and hardware store, having a public funeral for the child was the only instance of Carol defying her husband. His demand to bury the child quietly and minimize the shame of her not having been right was intolerable to Carol. She went to the priest who understood her need, and a funeral and dinner were held. As far as anyone knew, Carol's husband never mentioned the child again.

Carol had dabbled in other business interests prior to her McDonald's job. When her children began to leave home, she spent some time in the Tupperware business, followed by a stint with Amway. Her husband objected to her being involved in sales, however, proclaiming loudly at one family reunion that there was no hell worse than having a wife who thought she could run her own business. In the same outburst, he admitted to demanding that Carol hand over any money she made to him because he had to hire someone to work evenings in the hardware store while Carol went, as he put it, begging door-to-door. Carol said nothing about her business to anyone except to observe at her sixty-fifth birthday party that she was retiring from the hardware store. Though he had never given her the actual paycheck, Carol's husband had, on the advice of his accountant, entered her on the payroll, making her eligible to draw her own Social Security. About the time her husband inherited the land, Carol began receiving small checks that covered her meager necessities. The Social Security income made her McDonald's job even more curious. Why *did* Carol clean tables?

I never gave much thought to Carol's career choices, though I was impressed by the degree of the consensus about the ill temper of her husband and about the quiet, hardworking style of Carol's life. It was, then, a surprise to me when one day in the grocery store, she pulled me aside. Rather urgently, she asked me if I would be attending a dinner at the church the following weekend. When I told her I would be there, she asked me to stop by the kitchen where she would be working. "There is something that I want to give you," she said, and without further words, she pushed her cart down the aisle and away from me.

When I saw her again she was standing by the huge sink in the parish kitchen, scrubbing out a coffee pot. She wiped off her hands and reached under the counter, grabbing her pocketbook. Opening it quickly, she took an envelope and put it in my hand, saying, "I know that you know a lot of missionaries — please send this to someone who can use it. And don't worry about writing a note to thank me." She quickly closed her pocketbook and went back to her scrubbing. I put the envelope in my own purse and left the kitchen, not realizing that I had just become one of the conduits through which Carol would give away her money from McDonald's and, in so doing, say "I Am" to the world.

I didn't open the envelope until I got home. Inside it I found a pile of crisp twenty-dollar bills. After some discussion, my husband and I decided to divide the money between two friends who worked in Peru. We made arrangements for the money to get to them without getting into details about its origin.

Two letters of acknowledgment quickly came back to us. The first was from a woman who worked with a group dedicated to improving health conditions, no small task in a country where access to vaccinations and basic medical care is limited by severe economic inequality. The group engaged women in a number of creative and empowering projects, including classes that taught the basics of preventive health care and the use of natural remedies; immunization programs; and several nutrition projects. More than anything else, however, the group practiced a philosophy that health is a human right and that dignity is a vital component of healing. We thought that the group would be an appropriate recipient of the money that Carol earned, quietly and on her own. The letter said:

> Thank you for sending the money. The economic situation here is absolutely desperate. Each day I ask myself how people can survive the worsening conditions. There is, in the midst of all of the desperation, cooperation and care, but it's tough going. The women's health project is so short on funds that we are raising money by selling cooking oil in the market. Yet the classes and commitment go on. We used the money you sent to buy benches for the women to sit on during the classes. It is an investment that will last a long time, and it's something that we've desperately needed. So, thank you, and thank your anonymous donor.

Through my friend, we passed the message to Carol that her money had bought benches for the women's group. I could not help but think of the benches as a symbolic link between women whose lives had given them few opportunities to rest, yet who retained the courage to reach out to each other.

The second letter we received was from a priest working with people newly arrived in one of Lima's shantytowns. The people had worked hard to build a small chapel. In addition to providing a gathering space, in the midst of their precarious reality, the small chapel also served as a powerful symbol that both God and the people were in this place to stay. Joe, the priest, wrote:

> After all these months and years of slow work and lots of change, we finished the chapel in the newer part of the neighborhood. We celebrated Mass and then had a wonderful party. There was lots of singing and dancing and eating that went far into the night. Once again I saw and learned from the powerful ability of people to experience and celebrate joy, even as life here is so very hard. The money you sent bought some of the last materials we needed. Thanks for the gift. It will last a long time.

It was ironic that the fruits of Carol's leap of independence from the hardware store had bought cement and nails to complete a chapel. The next time I saw Carol happened to be in the back of church. When I whispered that her gift had helped furnish a place to pray, she smiled and thanked me for telling her.

Our next contact with Carol came in the form of a box of hand-knit hats that confirmed my suspicion that we were not the only avenue for her giving. It seemed that a workshop for physically and mentally challenged people had undertaken a special knitting project. Carol found out about the project and, with her money from McDonald's, bought every hat they made. She dropped off hats at charities all over the city. It was the dead of winter, and, as she told me, the hats were thick and bright and maybe could keep someone warm. She thought that we could help her distribute the hats. Remembering the sad story of her daughter, we were happy to accept and distribute the hats. We gave them to someone who worked in a shelter for homeless men. At Carol's invitation, we kept one for each of our sons.

Several months passed before we heard from Carol again. We learned from my friend that Carol's husband had decided to retire and travel the country in a Winnebago. Some time later, we were seated near them at a church potluck supper when the subject of the travel plans was raised. Carol sat silently while her husband went on about the advantages of seeing the countryside. He then poked fun at Carol, saying with a snicker that it was more important for her to live in the same old house than to see the world. "Besides," he said with obvious sarcasm, "she doesn't want to give up her job." A few days after that comment, we received another envelope from Carol, filled with crisp twenty-dollars bills and her usual request to pass the money on to someone who needed it.

That time we sent the money to a priest who worked in the Peruvian Altiplano. We knew from his letters that bad weather and a worse economy had created many needs; we also knew he would distribute the money with wisdom. His letter told the story:

There is a woman in town who was abandoned by her husband. She has four children, the youngest of whom is severely crippled. Needless to say, she suffers greatly. A few months ago, her home was destroyed by a flash flood. The people of the parish, who are themselves so poor, took up a collection to help her replace her home. It was powerful and humbling to see so many people make their offerings from what they had to live on. The money you sent bought beds, pots, and a few other major items. It was a most generous and timely gift.

It was a gift given from all of the dignity that Carol had to live on.

The last gift we received from Carol came during the cholera epidemic in Peru. We forwarded the money to people who were working day and night to stop the epidemic; Carol's donation bought medicine and printed materials. The note we received from our friend captured the urgency of the epidemic:

> Thank you for the money. The cholera is as horrible as you've heard. We do what we can.

I told Carol about the medicine, and again she smiled.

After that donation, we never heard from Carol again. Her husband's plans for a perfect retirement took her away in a Winnebago; she could not resist him on this. Before they left, Carol told lots of people, including those who speculated most about her, that she would pray for them. It was a promise she undoubtedly kept. Eventually Carol and her husband settled in a retirement village where life is perfectly structured. According to my friend, Carol is working again at a restaurant, and no one can understand why she would bother. I am certain that in her new surroundings, Carol has found recipients for her mite.

If I had the power to rewrite Carol's life, I would change almost every aspect of it. There is an element of sadness in the picture I have of her washing tables at McDonald's, her dyed hair carefully tucked under a hat designed to be worn by teenagers. I wish that she could have gone to school, had not lost her daughter, had a husband who treated her well. I wish that she had been able to live with a sense of dignity and autonomy all of her life. I wish that she knew more fully her own beauty and potential. Likewise, I wish that there were no children dying in poverty, no epidemics, no shacks perched on the side of inhospitable hills. My wishes, however, are not life's reality. As sad and enraging as that reality is to observe, I must respect the way in which the soul finds ways of surviving it. Carol's life and the connection she made through her charities illuminate elements of the soul that are as common in human experience as is her captivity.

I am aware that Carol's charities can be interpreted in a number of ways, one of those being that in her giving she participated in her own exploitation. I prefer to understand Carol's actions as an outgrowth of compassionate faith. A woman whose identity had been suppressed her entire life made a connection to the world by quietly building a bridge between herself and others who suffered. Carol found a dignity no one could take from her by choosing her charities and, reaching beyond herself, letting her spirit be visible in the world. She did it quietly and without expectation of acknowledgment. Like the women who sat on the benches she bought, Carol had few opportunities for rest, yet she could be a co-creator of a better world.

Carol's jobs outside the home and the hardware store, culminating in her job at McDonald's, gave her dignity and control that she experienced nowhere else in her life. While she, in fact, did not need the money, she most assuredly needed the sense of dignity that is vital to healing. Once Carol began receiving checks that bore her name, she practiced works of mercy that created places of rest and worship. The job and its proceeds were all that Carol had to live on for a sense of herself as separate and independent. The saddest, and yet most hopeful, theme of her story has to do with commonality. She deepened her dignity by assisting people whose suffering, though on the surface quite

different, was linked to her own. From her pain, she reached beyond herself to people whose names she did not know but whose
need she quietly, deeply, and compassionately understood. Carol
acted on the redemptive need to imagine a better world.

CHAPTER THREE

Death in the Night

*Though they walk through the Valley
of the Weeper,
they make it a place of springs
clothed in blessing by the generosity
of early rains.*

—PSALM 84:7

F OR THE LAST THIRD of his life, my father was not healthy. Knowing of his several heart attacks, bad circulation, and lungs compromised by years of smoking, I did not think of him as having the potential for a long life; that he had lived to be sixty-one was something of a miracle. He had about him, however, a certain sense of immortality that was buttressed by his size and appearance of strength. My father stood six feet two inches with broad shoulders and a grip of steel. He had survived much in his life, including World War II, a plane crash, and countless trips to cardiac care where he would, for all the world, look like he was dying only to leave the hospital a few days later and resume his life. The pattern of his illness came to be familiar; over time I had stopped consciously worrying that he would drop dead, though the fear that crept through me when he was late returning from a business trip or when he slept too soundly led me to know that the vulnerability of his heart never really left my mind.

Those being my images, at least for the last several years of his life, it was a precious gift that in his last few hours, he seemed remarkably healthy and happy. He came to do business and to visit me in a town where I was living, three hours from home. For the three days he was with me, his face, so often frighteningly gray, was full and bright with life. He laughed easily and often, as if some unseen burden had been lifted from him. When he wasn't working, we spent time shopping and eating in various restaurants. It was mid-June, and the world was in bloom. Several times we drove along the Mississippi River, enjoying a happy, relaxed time filled with conversations that brought words together in ways that were surprisingly revealing, especially for my father. Throughout the visit, he was full of stories and comments about what he had learned in life. There seemed to be a lot that he wanted to tell me in the space of days we had together, an urgency of communication that I welcomed like an unexpected guest.

One evening we drove to a fishing camp for supper. The camp restaurant sat on the edge of the Mississippi with huge windows looking out on the river's rapid and powerful flow. Above the windows were stuffed bass that had been pulled from the river and suspended on the wall as if at any moment they might come to life and jump back in the water. I told my father that their presence made me want to eat chicken. He laughed. He told me not to think too deeply about food sources and ordered a steak. We watched heavy barge traffic as we ate. The grace of the barges led my father into a series of comments about transportation, the power of the river, and ultimately into recollections about the navy.

The war was an unusual thing for him to talk about, yet that evening he described it with emotion. He talked about the irony of World War II giving his life meaning and order even as it created so much chaos in the world. He commented on the widespread feeling that the war was a just cause, a feeling that gave energy to those who fought in it. There was still discernible pride in his sense of victory. He then talked about the great sorrow he felt when he saw pictures of the cities that had been devastated by Allied bombs. He'd flown over those cities, he said, and during some of his time in the Pacific, he had navigated planes that dropped their cargo and then quickly flew away. He knew that there had been great suffering in it all and that too many people died. For that, he said, we must all be sorry, and he shifted in his chair as if to chase the memories of the losses back into hiding.

While he was talking, the weather began to change. We could see the barges stop moving in anticipation of a storm that was whipping up intensely. It was suddenly raining so hard that we could not see the river through the sheets of water and punishing wind. "I guess we'd better have dessert," Dad said. While the storm frightened those caught on the river, we passed the time in a level of conversation that was curiously deep and comforting. One-by-one he talked about each member of the family; his pride in my mother, my sisters, and my brother was obvious as he spoke. He talked at length about little things, about furniture and cars and vacation trips, which eventually led to comments about gratitude and blessings in life. My father talked about the way he remembered each of us from childhood: Ann knitting when she was four, Beth playing with the dog, my habit of pushing around a coffee can in my doll carriage, Nick playing with his toy lawn mower. In the poignant images of his memories, he revealed a love that sometimes had been difficult for him to express in words. When he talked about the wonder of having become a grandfather, tears filled his eyes, and he said, "It is the greatest thing that has ever happened to me." And then he said that there was nothing in life that meant more to him than each of us, and that when he looked at his granddaughter, he felt his life was fulfilled. The conversation had a feeling of completeness, as if I was unwittingly receiving the testimony of my father's life in a moment that, as I was living it, appeared as ordinary as a June rainstorm. And, indeed, that was precisely what was happening.

The storm ended as quickly as it had begun, and the sun suddenly lit the sky in the brilliant colors of an evening close to the summer solstice. The windows of the car were open while Dad drove me home, and we commented on the freshness of the air and the gentle breezes that had replaced harsh winds. As he turned the corner by my home, Dad drove through a huge puddle. The water splashed into the car and soaked him. First I bit my lip and tried to give him his dignity by not laughing at the sight of the muddy drops running down his arm. We both knew, however, that dignity and control were lost causes. "Go ahead and laugh. I guess it's funny," he said. And then I laughed hard, and he laughed too, and we said that it had been a nice night. When he dropped me off, we made plans for breakfast, and he drove back to his hotel to change his shirt, our parting being the laughter that, in the end, neither of us could contain.

At 1:30 in the morning, I got a phone call from the house doctor of the local hospital. He told me that my father had suffered a serious heart attack and that I should come to the intensive care unit as quickly as I could. I threw on my clothes and grabbed my raincoat because the storm had returned, and this time I was not to be protected from its viciousness. Dark torrents of rain washed away memory and hope of morning as I struggled to drive in the storm. When I arrived at the hospital, I was met by the doctor and a priest who had been called at my father's request. They told me that my father was in cardiac shock and that he would most certainly die, probably within the hour. The priest told me that he had anointed my father. When I told him that, though he had recently been taking instructions, Dad wasn't Catholic, the priest cleared his throat and said that we could receive him into the church, thus swiftly and rather unceremoniously taking care of countless childhood prayers for my father's conversion.

When I saw my father, there was no question in my mind that we were to have moments, not hours, together. The priest and I prayed, and I held my father's hand and struggled with the words of a familiar prayer, choking on the phrase, "Our Father who art in heaven..." I knew that these were to be the prayers of passage, and I was grateful that the church had words and ways of giving a comforting structure to hold my spirit when my whole world was falling apart.

It all happened quickly; it took forever; it was peaceful; it was terrifying; it was a gifted moment that has, nonetheless, burdened me with its memories and meaning. It was my father's deathbed. At first he knew I was there; then comprehension faded away with the loss of blood to his brain; then he didn't recognize my presence; then he was afraid; and then he was dead. Finally, in the silence of the intensive care unit, there was a great peace that I could not cherish because there was so much to do. My father had just died before my eyes in the middle of the night. There was within me a child's hope that if I didn't tell anyone or begin to tend to the necessary details, none of it would be true; for a brief moment I wanted to run out into the rain, keeping the night's events in the place of bad dreams. A storm was raging outside, a storm was raging inside, and I was suddenly confronted with a series of questions and decisions that I dealt with in the midst of overwhelming feelings and a desperate need to be quiet.

The kindness of strangers — the doctor, the nurses, the funeral director, the priest — gave me strength to hold reality, with its precious and painful elements, in my heart. The priest drove me home, where I was met by a friend who stayed with me while I called my family in another state, startling them from their sleep with sad news we had all long expected and still found shocking. Because it was so near the solstice, morning light came early and surprised me. It seemed unbelievable that the sun could rise after so raw and deep an experience of night. I could not fathom that the cycle of life continued in the day or, bound as I was in a cycle of terror, loss, and grief, that there could ever be a sense of wholeness and resurrection. That morning I took some of the money from my father's wallet, and he posthumously bought breakfast for the friends who had gathered to be with me; union, communion, the very concrete experience of love and the surprise of morning light.

The next few days were rich with the kind of lessons I was blessed to learn relatively early in life. In moments of grief one knows the family to which one belongs, and my father's funeral was a powerful experience of being connected to a large circle of people who truly cared and who had all been touched in some way by my father's life. There was a sense of nurturance and, surely, resurrection. The possibility of life from death felt as concrete as the presence of the people who came to pray and sing with us at the funeral and share our memories and our pain.

And still, the pain was wrenching and made surreal by a lack of sleep and constant stimulation. I felt exhausted and mute. The most desolate moment of the passage was the night after the funeral when the crowds had gone and the emptiness settled upon the house. It was then that I knew grief would not be neatly handled or wished away from my heart. I had been completely transported in a few moments from the innocence of knowing death as an abstraction to the actual experience of witnessing my father's passage to another world — one minute accessible, the next minute gone, taking with him the luxury of thinking that there would always be more time or another reprieve from death.

I soon found that I had used up my culturally allocated time for grieving, and the emptiness of my days intensified the heaviness in my heart. I had planned to spend most of July visiting a diocesan mission parish in Bolivia. The initial exhaustion after my father's death made me wonder if I was up for that kind of adventure. As the empty summer days stretched before me, however, I began to think that travel to a distant place would, at least temporarily, take away the pain of death in the night. I began to sense that it might be fortunate that, in the midst of my grief and exhaustion, I had a plane ticket to a completely different place eight thousand miles away. For want of an alternative plan, I took my tender heart to the airport and began a long journey, no longer filled with the questions about mission and church that had originally motivated the trip, but empty and aching with the freshness of loss that was reordering my world.

Instead of my grief being forgotten in Bolivia, it fast became a point of entry into a surprising new relationship with life. The journey through a nation ravaged by poverty and loss brought me home to a knowledge that the human heart, in its grief and its joy, is a universal and awesome gift. I experienced and celebrated that commonality in actions as simple and profound as joining in the dancing at a wedding, buying fruit at the market, and receiving Eucharist in a dark church where I stood next to a woman dressed in mourning clothes. In those places I began to understand the incarnation; the courage of the Bolivian people to live, love, and laugh in spite of overwhelming adversity made it easier for me to recognize the presence of God in my own experience of pain and loss.

While I was in Bolivia, the people were tormented by a violent, well-organized military coup intended to break the national spirit. While I, at home, had carefully read books to prepare for the trip, the military and paramilitary forces in Bolivia had been carefully composing lists of their enemies. The worst elements of the military drove tanks into the streets of La Paz and declared a new national order. Within a few hours, leaders of labor movements, people connected with the Catholic Church, and reporters were taken to detention centers where they were viciously tortured. In a mining town that had a well-organized labor movement, a thousand people were murdered in two days.

Newspapers ran pictures of tanks in the streets. The powerful, intimidating presence of the military left no question about who was in charge of the country or how much violence would be inflicted to maintain the new order. Any sign of organization or empowerment was to be eradicated. The church—which had begun loudly to proclaim God's care for the poor — not only had become suspect for the first time in Bolivian history but was publicly named as an enemy of the regime. There were no newspaper pictures of the sinister movements by night—paramilitary forces driving ambulances through the city and snatching that night's enemies of the regime. National stadiums held political prisoners at the mercy of a regime that intended to break all resistance and stay in power for a long, long time.

All of us at the mission were a bit unnerved by having met and danced with people who were, a few days later, hiding in fear for their lives. The coup happened close up to people we knew — however briefly — and that gave it an immediacy and a horror that altered the soul. Evil itself had immediacy: first in the crushing, death-inflicting poverty and then in the coup that murdered thousands and, within a few weeks, made drug trafficking the backbone of the Bolivian economy.

Returning to the United States, I discovered that it was amazingly difficult to convince anyone in Washington or the media that a coup in Bolivia was important news or that there was any reason to care about what was happening to people in such a distant place. None of it, I was told, was directly connected to

U.S. interests. I was constantly reminded that there was nothing I could do, and a few people tried to comfort me with a promise of forgetfulness; with time, they said, the images of my father's death and the poverty and violence of Bolivia would surely fade from consciousness. They did not.

When autumn came, I moved to Chicago, where I began graduate school and tried to make sense of personal sorrow and political upheaval. I studied hard, had a part-time job, participated in a human rights committee, and wavered between trying to make the summer's memories holy and trying blindly to make work my comforter. Many nights, after exhausting myself with my human rights meetings and my books, I was haunted by images of my father's last minutes. The hope that Dad had gone to a better place was usually too distant to be comforting; those nights I recalled our laughter on the night he'd been drenched, and I felt an immediate connection to my father in the blessing of those few summer days when he truly was as happy as I had ever seen him.

Only with the mercy of the years have I begun to understand that the images of my father's deathbed and the first, startling trip to Latin America are being made whole through prayerful attentiveness. In the last days of my father's life, I was given a chance to see the world as he viewed it, quickly, like a snapshot that could hold only a single moment. Yet the giving of that picture and the events that followed turned out to be the basis for understanding life as interconnected and full of mystery. When I went to Bolivia, I met sorrow face-to-face; I could neither shut out nor escape the realities of my own life because the suffering of others made it impossible for me to ignore the agony in my heart. From that place of divine compassion, a calling to cherish life was born.

My father's death and my first trip to Latin America, happening as they did within a few weeks of each other, handed me a complex and beautiful piece of fabric from which I continue to take pieces for my life's comforter. Some irretrievable innocence was left behind in the direct experience of death giving way to life. With the loss came a longing to live faithfully and with integrity in a grossly divided, violent world. It was that longing that led me to return to Latin America to live. I again experienced there the surprise of morning light; the grace of God manifest in hope present in the midst of pain, the cycle of life being filled with resurrection. I would come to marvel at a faith that defies imagination, at a gift of grace that, in the words of a popular Bolivian idiom, "can only be seen with eyes that have cried." And to my surprise, those tears became a baptismal blessing.

CHAPTER FOUR

The Journey

I, it is I who comfort you.

—ISAIAH 51:12

T HE RAGGED RED BUS traveled under a brilliant sky sliced by the sharp outlines of the Andes Mountains. The bus was filled beyond capacity as it headed toward the main streets of Cochabamba. Passengers pushed one another to enter the bus, then pushed one another again to exit it. Only the people who had entered the bus at the beginning of the route were seated, and they were trapped in their places by the crowd. People were pressed tightly against their neighbors, elbows inflicting injury, feet constantly caught under the crushing step of a fellow passenger. By the time the bus neared the center of the city, those wanting to ride held on to the outside of the bus, their hands grasped around window and door frames, their lungs taking in the raw fumes of the bus. When Bolivian buses have accidents, and they frequently do, the people hanging on the outside die first, crushed by the weight of a vehicle that symbolizes its passenger's lack of alternatives.

Riding with faces pressed against the back of another person, on a dangerous, smelly bus, is part of the daily experience of those who are poor. Sometimes when the day is warm, the air on the bus particularly fouled by fumes, or the crowd more compressed than usual, the frustration of the people erupts in small fights over the available small spaces. This was such a day. Words were sparse but sharp: "Watch out." "Move over." "This is my space." Passengers alternately yelled at the driver to slow down, speed up, watch where he was going, stop, don't stop. The driver responded to their complaints by swearing and honking the horn.

As the bus passed through the center of town, the crowd thinned to the point that no one was left hanging on the outside of the bus. The inside of the bus, however, was still crowded enough to make each arriving or departing passenger the cause of conflict. At one stop, a small woman carrying an infant wrapped in a bright red and blue woven cloth pushed her way onto the bus. Since there was no place for her to sit, she stood next to the driver, clutching the baby. More people wanted to enter the bus, and they pushed her forward, causing her to struggle and reach for a passenger's arm to catch her balance. When people told her to move out of their way, she did not respond. The crowd pushed against her, but there was nowhere for the woman to go. Tears began to flow down her cheeks as she stood silently holding her baby in the midst of the frustrated crowd. Slowly people quieted as they recognized the intensity of her crying. After a few wordless moments in which the woman's tears absorbed her voice, she quietly said, "The baby is dead."

Once she had spoken those words, her story began to spill out in the halting language of a heart that is enduring sorrow too profound to be evenly described. The baby girl had become sick the previous day with violent dysentery. The woman lived in an area where medical care was not immediately available. As soon as it was possible, she caught a bus into the city to seek assistance. By then the baby was very weak and could no longer nurse. When she arrived at the public clinic, the woman saw that there were many mothers and many sick babies that day. Judging by the size of the crowd, she knew that it could take hours for her to see the doctor. She sat in the crowded waiting room, hoping desperately that her baby could be helped, unable to get access to anyone who could help her baby be seen sooner. While awaiting her turn, the infant quietly died. Without saying anything, the mother wrapped her red and blue cloth around the baby and walked out of the hospital, never having seen a doctor or nurse. Everyone knew what had happened next. She stood on the street corner and waited for the bus, numb with exhaustion and grief, having no choice but to get on the broken, crowded bus to tenderly carry her dead baby home.

As the woman spoke, the sounds on the bus changed from people complaining about the ride to the soft murmur of people acknowledging a pain too familiar in that part of the world. Each heart understood the enormity of the suffering and the powerlessness it represented. A man stood up and gave his seat to the mother. Those who had a few minutes earlier been speaking harshly to one another shared words of comfort and compassion with the mother and among themselves.

Several people quietly said, "What a shame," while others murmured among themselves, "What pain." "It is better now," offered one woman firmly.

"Yes," said another woman, "the baby is an angel now."

"It is God's will," someone said with certainty. "The baby has been spared all of the suffering on earth."

People shook their heads in agreement and fell silent. The mother held her baby and cried with a constancy that suggested hers was a sorrow too deep to yet yield to visions of angels or promises of a better life. As new passengers entered the bus, they were quickly told what had happened, their heads turning to nod at the mother and acknowledge her loss. When the bus reached her stop, the woman stood up carefully and carried her baby off the bus. Passengers looked out the window and watched her walking toward her house, the lifeless bundle pressed against her chest. The woman's family and neighbors would help her prepare the baby for burial. She was too poor to buy one of the tiny white coffins for sale in the town market; her baby would be wrapped in a cloth and placed in a tiny grave split out of the rocky soil. Sadly, it would not be difficult to find someone who had experience breaking the earth to receive the body of an infant; this baby girl was certainly not the first in the area to die.

"It is God's will," someone repeated as the bus pulled away from the stop. "It is better now." And finally, quietly, someone said again, "What pain." Then there were no more words. As people who had shared the mother's journey exited the bus and new passengers entered, the silence of the mother's great sorrow was replaced by the sounds, and the frustrations, of people going about their lives. As life's noises filled in the void, the assurance that the death of the baby was the will of God, and, indeed, an act of mercy, hung in the air with the wrenching image of a dead baby girl held to her mother's chest. Hanging with it was the hope that there was mercy in the suffering of both mother and child and an explanation of God's will in so horrible a pain.

Those of us who had come to Latin America as missioners hoping to share a message of hope found ourselves confused by the reality of the suffering mother and the conclusion that it was God's will that the baby die. There was nothing in our direct experience, or our years of study, that helped us understand the depth and commonality of that kind of pain. We talked about the desperation of the social situation and the historical antecedents of the notion that the suffering of the poor is an act of God, but we could reach no conclusions that reframed the mother's sorrow so that it might be explained in either human or theological terms. It was simply a horrible glimpse of the pain and indignity suffered day after day by those who are poor. In the face of that reality, our notions of divine presence and will were distant constructs of a language that no longer captured our experience; our anxiety was that we had no other words of comfort.

Palm Sunday fell in the following week. Before leaving the city for a day at a retreat house in the countryside, my husband and I attended a liturgy at the downtown cathedral. It was a long Mass, full of prayers; people reverently reenacted the entrance into Jerusalem; a reading of the Passion brought to my mind the clear image of the woman with the dead baby. That week a radio announcement, sandwiched between two musical selections, had asked people to donate money to assist in the burial of children. It was very clear that the toll of a worsening economic crisis was being exacted in suffering and death, particularly of those whose bodies had the least reserves to fight against diseases hunger breeds. There had been a lot of discussion among pastoral agents about the best response to the crisis, but no single answer emerged, beyond the recognition that none of us had the resources to fix things. In the dark air of the cathedral, I thought about the dying children, the horrible suffering, and a passion that seemed to have no end. Listening to the Gospel account of Jesus' suffering, it was easier for me to comprehend the feeling of abandonment than it was to understand the concept of placing one's spirit in God's hands.

After the liturgy we left the cathedral and went to the market to buy food for our journey. It was another clear and beautiful day in which the blue sky stunningly framed and defined the mountains. There was a great contrast between the solemn darkness inside the cathedral and the bustle of the marketplace. Communicating with sign language, we bought fruit from a woman who spoke only Quechua. She looked very tired sitting there, and she appeared to be blind. A few medical names for what was troubling her sight flashed through my mind, a defensive response to the awareness that the suffering of this one woman held in its intensity the suffering of an entire people. As we turned away from the woman and her pile of pears, a man walked by with a tiny white coffin tied to his back with a bright woven cloth. I felt my heart race. Focusing on the clarity of the mountains against the sky, I wondered, as I had many times before, how there could be so much beauty and so much pain in the same place. And I wondered why God had forsaken this long-suffering people.

We caught a ride on a market bus that was leaving the city. It was hot and uncomfortable, but we were able to sit down. Most of the other people on the bus were returning home after selling their produce in the marketplace. They had left their homes before dawn and, having carried their heavy loads into the market, needed rest. The bus lumbered along the mountain road, bumping against stray rocks and causing jostling that only occasionally drew comment from the tired passengers. As we traveled, the man sitting next to me fell asleep with his head resting on my shoulder. His face wore the weariness of that particular Palm Sunday, combined with the exhaustion of a lifetime in which he had labored hard and received few monetary rewards. A few times he stirred, picked up his head, and said, "Forgive me, Senora; I am so sorry." His apology and his gentle face soon yielded again to sleep.

The sleeping man wedged me into the seat. Trying hard not to disturb him, I read an article in the international edition of *Newsweek* about the need for tough economic policies in countries with outstanding foreign debts. That week the president of the United States had told the president of Argentina to demonstrate "political will" and make tough choices for his country. These choices included devaluation of the local currency, refinancing of the debt at higher interest, lifting of import-export controls, and tight control of labor movements. That the complexity of the financial issues could be reduced to a matter of political will was startling. I began to feel sick, presumably from reading on the bumpy bus, but, perhaps more accurately, from the staggering presence of too many irreconcilable realities in the world around me. I put down the magazine, again being careful not to awaken my seatmate. Resting against my leg was the man's empty market bag, which he held in his calloused fingers even as he slept. I wondered what the concept of "political will" meant to this man's life. Would such will and its subsequent choices lead to his death? And, as disturbing, is there a way in which political will and the will of God can easily become confused?

We passed by the reservoir for the city, its sparkling beauty defying the fact that a lack of money for water treatment had turned the reservoir into a pool of germs. Next to the reservoir was an army installation. That particular regiment had been called upon frequently to enforce order, sometimes with very cruel means. The soldiers had kept dictators in power, had ended strikes in the tin mines by shooting the strikers, had participated in all forms of repression, and most recently had been called upon by the international community to patrol the flow of coca leaves out of the jungle. The soldiers had marched to these scenes of violence along the very road we were traveling on. Everything looked quiet that day, the reservoir holding its germs silently, a place of torture looking like a series of well-kept buildings. My feelings of nausea increased; my seatmate slept. Just past the reservoir I gingerly woke the man and asked his permission to pass in front of him. He smiled and apologized again for his exhaustion; I smiled and said that I really didn't mind.

As Dick and I were leaving the bus, some confusion developed. The bus driver changed his price three times, and he sighed when he had to repeat the final amount. As we reached for the money to pay the fare, the man sitting directly behind the driver said, "Take whatever they will give you. They're gringos; they don't know anything." Several people sitting around the man laughed. We gave our money to the driver and departed, feeling humiliated by the man's remark. But as we walked along the road, we admitted to each other that in a very real way the man was right. What did we really know of the depth of suffering and the depth of inner resources experienced by the people around us? Would we ever be faced with the prospect of getting back on a crowded bus with a dead baby? Did we directly know what it means to struggle each day for bread? Did we really understand the depth of the Passion from the perspective of someone who lived its truths without the insulation of words or familiar constructs? And if, indeed, we knew nothing of those lived realities, what did it mean to live and share faith with those who did?

Those questions were not yet so carefully formed as we walked toward the retreat house under the clear, defining sky. What I was most aware of in the moment was the depth to which haunting, living images of the Passion had touched and disturbed my heart, giving me cause to wonder about the God to whom Jesus commended his spirit. I felt the incongruity of the discussions and debates held in comfortable living rooms, in which we observed the lack of a theology of the resurrection on the part of people who had suffered in ways that we, indeed, knew nothing about. That clear and beautiful Palm Sunday I began to question whether I knew or embraced the truth of the cross — living, unmitigated, and scandalous. I had been engaged in pastoral ministry that I understood as being rooted in the truth of the paschal mystery. Living in sight of people whose struggles and courage were beyond telling caused me to wonder if what I proclaimed was a promise of victory over death disembodied of the painful mystery of Christ crucified. Holy Week was shaped by that powerful question, and in place of a firm, clear answer, I found only the images of journeys by bus and the life revealed there.

We celebrated the Easter Vigil in a small parish church in Cochabamba. Of necessity, that night I was simply trying to be held by the power of the story of the Passion and the confident hope of resurrection. The Easter Vigil, with its wonderful readings and symbolic expressions, bonded the common faith story to the contradictions and sorrows around me, not as a means of understanding them or wishing them away, but as a reclamation of our common faith story. In the darkened church, somewhat daunted by the power of the liturgical rites and images — containing as they did so much of the truth I was struggling to accept — I asked myself why I ever thought I could clearly understand the will or mind of God. The haunting images of recent journeys led me to wonder about the implications of powerlessness resulting in the piercing of God's own flesh, not only in the historical moment of crucifixion but in the continuous human experience of profound suffering. It was a strangely comforting reflection that led to no conclusion beyond a new appreciation for the possibility that the presence of the Risen Christ might have forms I was too culturally bound to immediately recognize.

A few weeks after Easter, I participated in a discussion with a small Christian community. The catechetical materials for that particular meeting juxtaposed the words of Jesus, "I have come that you might have life and have it in abundance," with a story that the people in the group immediately understood. It described the death of an infant. A woman in the story said, "When the baby died, I thought it was a punishment of God." A powerful discussion of those two seemingly opposite statements followed. People talked about the experience of losing children, of the pain, and of the comfort offered them by other people. The phrases that had been said to the woman on the bus were repeated in the discussion: "It is a shame our babies die." "What a great pain." "It is better that the babies are angels." "Some of our children are special, so God takes them." "Sometimes we are punished."

Finally a woman said, "Our babies die not because God wants them to but because we have bad water. God wants us to have good water and keep our babies on earth. We have to work together to get good water." Her statement changed the focus of the group as it led to a discussion of the sorrow and oppression in their lives that came into being not because God willed it but because human beings sinned. That realization galvanized the group in an interesting and life-giving way. As one woman said with determination, "It isn't fair." The recognition of pain being caused by a lack of human justice was empowering for the group because it broke the link between God's will and the cause of the sorrow in their lives. If it wasn't God that was causing all of the pain, perhaps God would be with them as they struggled to find fresh sources of water.

The faith expressed by the woman in the small community created a space for understanding the will of God as not simply involving events, particularly those causing sorrow beyond telling, but rather as involving a way of knowing and being in the world. Her determination shifted the focus from a search for the will of God in a distant heaven to a claiming of God as the source of strength to work for justice on earth. God, she was quite confident, did not want the babies to die, and life and abundance were meant to be theirs. The energy that gathered in the group as they spoke was surely a moment of resurrection.

It is the will of God that we stand in the presence of great beauty and profound suffering and live our faith in action. The ability to grieve with one another and unite in the demand for pure water was an embodiment of God's will in the presence of mystery, sorrow, and pain beyond words. Life and abundance can thus pour forth from a rocky soil that holds the bodies of too many dead babies, and still blooms.

The invitation to live in that mystery, to commend one's spirit and actions to the living God, requires nothing less than embracing the suffering of the world and making it part of daily consciousness, recalling that God, too, suffers. Such an embrace does not come easily. What is required over and over again is changing our most basic beliefs and wishes about suffering and sin. Resurrection holds promise only when the suffering and sin are visible, felt, and received as an act of faith that makes it impossible to ignore the consequences of separation from the love and justice of God.

The woman who carried her dead infant onto the bus laid bare the heart of God in her weeping. That recognition, when felt on the level of the soul, makes the Passion of Jesus present in daily life, a presence that disturbs the heart by the truth of how much suffering is preventable. It also gives word to the deeper truth that hope can be born only in a heart that is attentive to suffering. Hope is not rooted in fantasy, control, or acts of will but in the radical proclamation that the cross is very real, a cause for scandal, and yet not the final word. Hope that is connected to the truth of the cross is compassionate and active; it forms the loving context from which one can live with a willingness to know both the sorrow and the joy of the human community.

In many ways, it was easier for me to keep a perspective on the reality of suffering and the presence of the cross when I was a foreigner in a strange land. Stripped of cultural props and understandings, there was nothing to insulate the hot wires of life, causing me to know with greater immediacy the profound need for human community. Without that community — and the experience of suffering that bound us together — I would have been stripped of the sense of connectedness that I needed in the loneliness of a cross-cultural setting. It is different for me now. These days most of my journeying is done on the commuter train into New York City, which, like most passengers, I ride in a way that is quite solitary. My greatest logistical concerns are securing a seat on the Hudson River side of the train and holding on to my coffee during station stops. The train ride is usually quiet and tranquil, as well-dressed people read their papers and generally ignore one another. No one on the train has ever fallen asleep on my shoulder, and I have certainly never seen the raw suffering that was present on that red Bolivian bus. I am not so simplistic as to think that the people around me are without pain. It is simply that in this place and time, we have more money to buy space and privacy that isolate suffering from daily consciousness.

I find it distressingly easy in my own country to isolate myself, to be less attentive to other people, and to create my own version of a theology that saves me from the darkness of questions I could not avoid in South America. Many days I rush through Grand Central Station without noticing its contrasts. I do not see the beauty of its high ceilings painted with the constellations or take note of the people sleeping near the stairs to the subway. In my haste I make the humbling discovery that my sense of compassion can be as much an outgrowth of my mood or time line as a fruit of spiritual discipline. Walking from one track to another in New York, it usually doesn't occur to me that there are great limits to what I know and understand of others' experience. I don't ask questions about the cross and the will of God for weeks at a time. I am again insulated, and it is easy not to look into the face of the suffering mother to understand the anguish of the Passion.

However, when I am honest with myself, I admit that I still carry the questions that rose in my heart on those earlier journeys into places of raw sorrow. I am less and less certain that I am supposed to put them to rest now, especially as life keeps teaching me the breadth of human suffering. I am continually called to be moved and disturbed by the tears of a heartbroken mother, the impaired sight of the woman in the market, the exhaustion of the man on the bus, not as images of distant memory but as a way of knowing what is important and redemptive in life. I am beginning to appreciate that where I stumble is on the truth that the only way to know God's will is to enter faithfully into the journey of life that unfolds in relationships and experiences that tear the heart and bring God's flesh to the world. The source of mercy and healing in life must surely be connected to the mystery of God's sharing the same fate as the beloved. The truth of the cross is meant to be disturbing, calling for attentiveness and personal connection in anonymous places so that the ravages caused by human choices are made visible.

The subtle yet powerful presence of God that was manifested in the shift of mood on the bus, the compassionate glances, the way people offered a word, any word, to alleviate a mother's great sorrow invites me to join the common struggle for life. It slows me down and makes me a more conscious traveler in an inattentive world. It is the will of the abundant God of life that a heart be woven that can collectively comprehend, remember, and share the pain of the Passion. Both the Passion and the heart to receive it have surprisingly simple and immediate expressions in the people's lives. Receiving those lives, and treating them with reverence, proclaims the hope of resurrection.

It is the will of God that we travel the common journey both haunted and hopeful, remembering and responding to one another's sorrows. I am certainly haunted by the images of suffering from the past, and, in my current environment, I become hopeful when I bring suffering to the light of consciousness, finding that it has a capacity to soften the heart and to bring Holy Week into ordinary time. The conversion occurs in the context of relationship — not simply with statistics and concepts but with human beings whose yearning for clean water in the here and now softens the hardest heart. And then I know for certain that God does not want the babies to die, that exhausted women and men should be relieved, that all water is not life-sustaining, and that the God of the resurrection weeps for the mother who is bereaved. In that union, God grants courage to dig new wells so that no more tiny graves will split the surface of the earth and tear the depths of a human heart. It is the will of God that we act according to the truth that, sooner or later, we all drink from the same reservoirs that contain within them the power of life and death.

CHAPTER FIVE

Of Bread and Bodies

I myself am the living bread come down from heaven.

—JOHN 6:51

L IFE CLINGS TENACIOUSLY to the unstable sand on the out-skirts of Lima, Peru. The city is surrounded by what are known as *pueblos jovenes* — young towns that have been settled over the years by people moving either from the countryside or more recently from other parts of the city itself, as refugees from economic and political hardship. Historically, the young towns have progressed toward organization and permanence, beginning with a settlement of tents and houses built of straw mats and moving toward stable housing and access to water and electricity. In more favorable economic times, people made that progression fueled by hope that built houses — one brick at a time. The economic reality of recent years has, however, left many people living permanently in straw houses perched on the sand with little protection from a world that does not value their lives. Hundreds of thousands of people live in these communities, with little access to medical care or municipal services. Life is pre-served by the tenacious hearts and actions of people who, while living on the margins of a large, modern city, refuse to be made invisible and so work hard, minute by minute, to build their community.

My husband and I moved to a young town, Pamplona Alta, to join a pastoral team that served approximately one hundred and fifty thousand people in a geographic area extending up the sand dunes as far as we could see. As part of a family catechetical program, we gathered in homes to pray and discuss Eucharis-tic themes. Sometimes the homes were built of brick, reflecting stability and the length of the owner's residence in Pamplona

Alta. Sometimes the straw mats that formed the fragile walls of the house held only the power of hope. Whatever the circumstances or external shape of the particular house where we met, the discussions and themes of the Eucharist were richly lived in a dialogue process that moved between Scripture and everyday examples and experience.

My initial excitement began to be tempered by the obvious difficulties of life in Lima's young towns. I began to wonder how people could retain faith in a place that seemed so desolate. Early each morning I was awakened by a little girl blowing a bicycle horn as she walked up and down the hills selling bread. She was so tiny and vulnerable that the purchase of bread from her made Eucharist seem more and more difficult to comprehend. The day-to-day suffering of people in the neighborhood took on new meaning as I learned the names and stories of people whose lives had been so profoundly defined by poverty, race, and gender. The violence of the area became more apparent, and I began to experience the insecurity of not knowing when I would be robbed or who I could trust in a country filled with the complexities of a struggle between terrorists and counterterrorists. I was learning to recognize the more subtle signs of malnutrition — the look in the eye, the shade of hair color, the shape of a stomach — that pointed to hunger of long standing. In one week, twenty-one babies died in one small part of the neighborhood. The people who participated in our catechetical meetings obviously knew these realities. Their lives had been shaped by events and struggles that I was only beginning to comprehend. I marveled at their faith, and I wondered sometimes at my lack of it.

The initial observations of the neighborhood and the pangs of my doubt came as I was experiencing the initial, transitional trimester when my first pregnancy was not yet obvious. There was no feeling of movement within, yet every system in my body was adjusting to the needs of the new life. I felt physically, emotionally, and spiritually thrown off balance. When one of the members of our pastoral team needed to return to the United States, I was asked to assume her role as an advisor to a neighborhood mothers' club. I felt totally unqualified to advise any group, let alone mothers, and was told that my role was simply to be with the women, listen to them, and provide a point of contact for the parish structures. Connecting with a group of mothers seemed like a very good idea as I was beginning to have all kinds of questions about childrearing, ranging from the most profound queries about mother/child bonding to mundane concerns about drying diapers under Lima's cloudy sky. I agreed to become the club's advisor, feeling in my heart that I could offer little more than my physical presence to the group.

The mothers' club meeting was held in a simple concrete building, the very existence of which gave witness to the spirit of the local community that had bonded together to construct it. My colleague met me at the door and walked with me inside to meet the women of the club. They were gathered in small groups, talking and laughing. A few women were scurrying about a long table of honor, setting places and moving large platters of food. Facing the table were three rows of simple wooden benches. Slowly women began to sit down on the benches, and I was, to my amazement, led to the table of honor and offered a place next to the president of the club. It was then that I learned that this was a special meeting of the mothers' club to say good-bye to their beloved advisor.

Through the president's moving good-bye speech, I learned of the many dimensions of the club. The women met for educational activities; they worked together to form a neighborhood soup kitchen; they participated in health-promotion campaigns and raised funds for social-service projects. But, as the president pointed out in her speech, their most important function was to be friends to one another. Sister Ann had been their friend, and she said they knew I would also be with them in their struggles and triumphs. She then announced that the banquet would begin. All of us at the table were served plates heaping with food. My nausea was working against me, a reality that Ann recognized. She said to the club president, "The senora can't eat much because she is pregnant," an announcement that was quickly shared with the group and met with genuine joy.

I ate as best I could, limited not only by my queasiness but by the reality that the women sitting on the benches received smaller portions of food than those of us at the table. I was being treated as an honored guest by women I had just met. I was deeply touched, and just as deeply ill at ease, in accepting their hospitality. I was being treated with a reverence that I found difficult to accept. The food placed before me was an expression of openness, appreciation, and love. In the midst of my doubt, my shattered sense of purpose, and the confusion wrought by my changing body, these women were offering me an invitation to embrace the presence of a God hospitable enough to make an offering of flesh.

One woman in the group caught my attention. Seated at the end of the first row, she seemed small and vulnerable. She was very thin, her body ground into the right angles of one whose hunger and hardship have been continual. As each course of the dinner was served, she took half of the food from her plate and put it into a series of plastic bags that divided her meal into now and later. She transferred the food quickly and purposefully. I was terribly moved as I watched her because it was obvious that she had made such transfers many times. I assumed that she was saving some of the food for her supper, which made me feel the power of her hunger. It would be some time before I understood that, in her hunger, this woman thought first of dividing her food with someone else. Her name was Clemencia. After the meal, she welcomed me to the group and said that she hoped to see me the following week. She said that she was happy to hear that I was going to have a baby. "A mother like us," she said and quietly walked away.

I returned the following week, without the security of having Ann at my side. A local women's group was conducting a series of classes for the mothers' club. An essential dynamic of the course was the women's exchange with one another about their experiences, their needs, their dreams, and their hopes. I was seated on a bench next to Clemencia. That day, she began to fill in the angles of her bones with the words of her story.

Clemencia had been born in Ayacucho, the area in Peru where the war of independence began 160 years earlier and where the most intense fighting between the insurgent group the Shining Path and military counterinsurgency was currently taking place. It was no accident that revolution had twice been born in Ayacucho since it is one of the most marginalized and neglected zones in Peru. When Clemencia was fifteen, her father gave her to a man in an arranged marriage, telling her that if she did not marry that man, she would be forbidden to marry anyone else. Marry him she did, but Clemencia told him she would let him know when he could come to her bed. She wept as she described his violent reaction to that self assertion. Eventually, Clemencia had been beaten enough. She took her small son and made her way over the mountains to Lima, where she sought a new life. Her resistance was an incredibly courageous act. She was alone in a difficult place, determined to care for her son. Clemencia made her home in one of the straw houses that would never be replaced by bricks. Yet, for Clemencia, those straw mats were a sign of independence. She struggled to raise her son by doing laundry for other people. Her son was then fifteen and, she said, laughing like the mother of any adolescent, hungry all of the time.

Each week as I returned to the mothers' club, I felt more and more at home there. The club became a place of safety where I was freed from the doubts and confusion that disturbed me in some of the more formal moments of my ministry. I participated fully in the course at the mothers' club, gradually learning more of the life story not just of Clemencia but of the other women gathered there. I learned that theirs were not hopes and dreams rooted in luxury; as one woman simply said, "What I most want is for my children to have enough to eat." Whenever food was served, I noticed that Clemencia quietly enacted her ritual of dividing her portion in half and slipping it into a plastic bag. After several weeks, she turned to me and said, "This is for my son." Then I understood that wherever she went, whenever she found food, Clemencia was conscious of the need to feed her child. Tending his hunger was never far from her mind.

My pregnancy was progressing, becoming much more obvious and much more difficult. I was discovering that sharing my body and blood with a baby, while a joyful experience, was also exhausting. I was retaining a lot of fluid, which swelled my extremities and made me very uncomfortable. The women in the club expressed concern not only for the physical difficulties of my pregnancy but for the fact that I was carrying my first child so far away from home. More than once they expressed to me their conviction that "a woman needs her mother and sisters when she is pregnant." They said that since I had no one from my family there, they would help me with the baby.

I was not the only woman in the club who was pregnant, and

the other expectant mothers were quickly becoming my sisters. We compared notes about how we felt, how much movement we experienced inside of us, and when our babies were due. Compared to the other mothers, I was huge. Clemencia overcame politeness and expressed amazement at the size of my stomach.

"Only one baby?" she said, holding up her index finger and looking at me quizzically.

"Only one," I replied.

"When will it be born?" she said, her arched eyebrow indicating that she was unconvinced that this was to be a single birth.

When I told her that I had four more months to go, Clemencia laughed and said, "You will fall over." We all laughed then, more attentive to what I was going to look like by the time of delivery than to the reality that a healthy baby with a normal birth weight was, by accident of geography and birth, more likely for me than for any of the other expectant mothers. The women spoke to me about the difficulties of carrying and delivering their first baby. I knew that their experience of obstetrical care was radically different from mine. Most of the women delivered in a hospital that would admit them only as the baby was about to be born. If there were any complications, they suffered them in the rawest form. The women around me knew only too well that to give birth is to pass through the shadow of death. They were all connected in some way to a woman who had been lost in childbirth. They knew too much about small babies, premature births, and early diseases. I feared for the pain and the unknown elements of childbirth, but I did not fear for my life or the life of my baby. That was the obvious difference between the other women in the mothers' club and myself. When we went through the birthing shadow of death, we had nothing less than five hundred years of history separating us.

While my baby grew inside me, the tumult of the Peruvian

economy made life even more difficult for the women in the mothers' club. The currency was devalued, unemployment rose, and the basic necessities of life were priced beyond the means of most Peruvians. For Clemencia, the economic chaos was particularly cruel, living as she did outside the margins of a marginated place; under the best of national circumstances hers was a difficult existence. The winds of the economic storm found her completely unprotected. She grew thinner still. Yet Clemencia kept her spirit, joining with other women in the neighborhood kitchens to make available one nutritious meal per day by pooling their labors and their resources.

I visited the kitchens and, in what felt like the only concrete contribution I made to the situation, put the women in touch with a diocesan program that helped them join a cooperative venture for buying food and cooking utensils. Dick and I continued to be involved in the catechetical program, and I continued to travel in my soul between the seeming opposites of awe and doubt. Many mornings I bought bread from the little girl on the street, my baby nourished by her labors. One Sunday morning, three women came to me after Mass with an offering of lettuce, the firstfruit of their desert garden, which they gave to me along with advice about eating food with lots of vitamins. I ate the lettuce and treasured the gesture.

My pregnancy was becoming more and more difficult as I entered the third trimester. I was showing all the signs of preeclampsia, a condition that can prove very dangerous for both the mother and child. The doctor was beginning to talk about the complications and raised the possibility of total bed rest for the remaining weeks of the pregnancy. It was becoming increasingly apparent that we needed to go back to the United States until the delivery. We were torn about the decision. I felt as though I was abandoning women who had become my friends and who did not enjoy my options. It was Clemencia who reminded me of the need for a woman to be with her own family when the time of delivery came. "Besides," she told me, "you carried the baby here, so it is always part Peruvian."

We did not have much time to get ready for our flight home. The next few days were a blur of travel agents and government officials stamping our passports to ensure that we could reenter the country with resident visas. I visited as many of the women as I could to say good-bye. Many of them gave me small gifts to carry with me and said to greet my family in their name. I had not, however, been able to find Clemencia.

The day before we left, I met her in the market. She looked exhausted, and as soon as I greeted her, she began to cry. Clemencia told me that the military was trying to illegally induct her son by accusing him of a petty crime, then offering military service as an alternative. It was a form of kidnapping that was, and is, all too common. Clemencia had been scrambling the past few days to prove that her son was too young to be hauled off into the mountains and trained as a counterinsurgent soldier. It was not an easy fight. She stood barefoot in the sand, crying, resistant, and defiant. Her tiny, work-worn hands were clenched in fists when she said to me, "They cannot have my son."

I had no doubt that Clemencia would bring her whole will to the fight with the military. She was resisting with the same courage that had brought her over the mountains with her son and had fed them both, bite-by-bite, day-by-day, for many years. Clemencia would struggle as she so often had with a determination that was truly self-transcendent. But there was little doubt in my mind that she would lose the fight and, most likely, ultimately lose her son. There was something in the nature of Clemencia's tears that told me she too understood that staggering truth. I stood silently with her while she cried, and I felt totally powerless. I was caught offguard when Clemencia wiped her tears and said to me, "Take good care of your baby." She touched my stomach with her tiny hands, and then she walked away.

When we arrived back in the United States, it was the dead of winter. The snow seemed to muffle all of the sad and joyous sounds of Pamplona Alta that we carried in our minds and souls. I was caught in a whirlwind of high-tech obstetrical care and culture shock. It was too difficult to describe Clemencia, the women in the mothers' club, the catechetical program, or the nature of my doubts, and so I simply did not try. My silence was not an attempt to obliterate those voices. It was instead a means of protecting the new life within me when energy was low and the demands on my body and spirit were too great for me to risk giving word to what had become for me the bread of life.

Several weeks after we left Lima, Michael was born in a high-risk and complicated Caesarean delivery that would have been radically different for the women from the hills outside of Lima. For me, everything needed for the procedure was readily available and disposable. Every possible backup was there, every contingency anticipated, every need met. As I was being taken to surgery, I remembered the terror women in Lima expressed at the possibility of a Caesarean. I was frightened, but I did not think I would die or be abandoned to suffer the pain in an unmitigated way. The doctor and nurses did what they could to retain the wonder of birth and were as gentle with me as circumstances allowed. I was grateful for their care, grateful for that accident of geography and birth.

When Dick handed me Michael in the recovery room, I was overcome with awe. Crying with relief and joy, I pulled back the blanket to look at him. The baby whose size had been a source of amusement to Clemencia, whose shape had been echoed in the shadow of a sonogram, whose heartbeat we had heard so many times in tests that scared us for their implications, was now in my arms. His head was shaped exactly like Dick's; his hands were miniatures of mine. We held him and embraced the beauty of what had been formed in darkness.

That night I experienced for the first time the reality that my body was created for communion. I was sleeping in my hospital room; Michael was sleeping in the nursery. I dreamed of him being hungry and needing me. I woke up and waited, not at all surprised to see the nurse appear at the door with my hungry, crying baby. That was to become a common experience — I would be sound asleep, would dream of Michael hungering, would awaken, and within a few minutes would be responding to his hungry cries. The dream always came first, as if my body and psyche worked together to meet the needs of my hungry infant. My body had become that of a mother, my breasts leaking milk at the sound of any baby's cry, my need to feed my child as immediate as breath. In a most basic way, I could no longer think of myself in only individual terms; my life was part of a nourishing whole.

It took me a long time to heal, which prevented our returning to Peru. Eventually the physical trauma faded into a neat scar at the base of my womb that was easily transformed into a fresh wound when the time came to deliver again. The silence about Clemencia and the experience in Peru deepened as I came to hold those memories all in my heart in a way that was not linear or easy to understand. While I lived as the source of nourishment and life for my baby, I felt connected to all women. It was as if the scalpel had cut not through my abdominal wall but through the veil of division that kept my world divided into those who were like me and those who were different, those truths of life I

78

could understand and those that were beyond me. I had dreams of my hungering infant; I had dreams of women trying to breast-feed in times of famine; and I knew that I could never again think of myself in terms that did not include relationship.

When illness and circumstances had made it necessary for us to leave Peru, we left a part of ourselves, and a great many belongings, in that place. Yet we took its blessings and, over time, made them as much a part of us as the scars of birth. Our experience in Peru was as profound and as difficult to describe as the communion between mother and child. It simply became the context for a new way of approaching life. We went about the business of reestablishing our lives in the United States, warmed by the excitement communicated from Peru after we had sent pictures and news of Michael.

When I first looked at Michael, I wondered what I was doing the day that his ears, fingers, and toes had silently formed. While I was waiting for the bus or hanging out the wash or asking questions about the meaning of Eucharist in a hungry place, creation had gone on within me, without my giving much conscious attention to the details. It was through an encounter with the process of life torn open and shared that God came to be revealed in my own physical experience. My body connected me to Meister Eckhart's image of God all day long on a birthing bed. God as a contracting womb, suffering, healing, preparing even in the midst of one birth to be poised for the reception of new life, made sense to me in a way that other theories and images did not.

That mystery was incarnated through Clemencia's torn and daily communion with her son. Those many plastic bags, and her determined stand, taught me that Eucharist, life, and love are quite concrete and indeed "a harsh and dreadful thing compared to the love in dreams." I am, as a result of Clemencia, a little less afraid of the communion born of sharing my body and blood, of the hospitality of those who labored for a torn piece of bread, and of saying amen to whole regions of life I cannot comprehend.

Clemencia and her son may both be dead now. The dirty war from which she tried to save him has taken many lives. Clemencia had nothing on her resistant bones to spare her from the latest rounds of hunger in Peru. From time to time I still dream of her. In my dream I am returning to Peru and trying to find her. When I make that journey, she is not living on the side of a sand dune but in a mansion. I have wondered sometimes if that mansion is the one prepared for her by God or if my unconscious simply cannot hold the reality of her courageous straw house. In any case, I know the dream to be a sign that Clemencia will always live for me in a silent, gestating place where interpersonal communion is as much the framework of life as is the angle of our bones. I carry her blessing, her words of friendship, and her instruction to take care of my baby. I pray to live faithful to the echoes of her life that show me God's form — the torn body making a precious ritual in each shared scrap of bread, the Body of Christ, present, living, and transformed beyond the tender margins of my doubt where faith mysteriously became visible as the source and sustenance of life.

CHAPTER SIX

Legacy

See, upon the palms of my hands
I have written your name;
your walls are ever before me.

—Isaiah 49:16

T HE WEEK that the cherry blossoms bloom in Washington, D.C., is filled with the magic of winter memories being healed by spring. Early on the first Sunday in April, I walked to the Tidal Basin to join the crowds breathing in earth's renewal. There were already a surprising number of people moving about with a spirit of lightheartedness and delight in the trees given by Japan as a sign of friendship and peace. The crowds walked under the fragrant canopy with spirit in their steps, the blossoms themselves a celebration. Discovering that they were unable to capture the fullness of spring in one photograph, many people chose a particular tree as the focal point of their remembrance. It was a happy crowd gathered there, the spirit of celebration enhanced by the joyous accompaniment of a brass band playing next to the Lincoln Memorial.

A few blocks away from the cherry trees, a different crowd had gathered to offer their chosen symbols as a sign of remembrance and a hope for peace. Within range of the sweet fragrance of the cherry blossoms, the Vietnam War Memorial was surrounded by a spirit quieter and more somber than that of those celebrating the blossoms, yet was no less a place of renewal and rebirth.

The memorial is simple. Shaped like a wide *V,* the shiny, black granite panels chronologically list the names of those who died in Vietnam. As one walks along the wall, the panels become larger until one reaches the deep center that reflects, in the burgeoning list of names, the height of the Vietnam War.

The memorial slices the earth like a deep wound, but it invites visitors into its center, and it holds them there in a unification of private and public grief. At the vortex of the memorial wall, the grief reflected in the individual names becomes a transformative plea for peace that is not to be understood simply in political terms. Rather, the wounded center grants its peace in exchange for reverent memory. The memorial is a rare place in American culture in that it creates a space for such a memory to be made visible. The memorial has a spirit of sacred tenderness that allows people to enact rituals of private grief in a public space.

The Vietnam War Memorial is a compassionate place. With few words exchanged between visitors, there is an understanding of respect and reverence. The Parks Department employees who stand along the wall speak in low, kind voices as they help people find names in directories that will lead them to the panel where letters engraved in stone give the massive loss of life a name. People wait in line quietly to use the directories, their profound feelings evident on their faces and in the fidgeting of their hands. The tear-streaked faces of people leaving the memorial are testimony to the power of all those losses. Held in those carved letters are memories of awful moments of notification that someone was missing or had died, the funerals, the burials of bodies, and emotions too raw to bear. The names hold the lost youth and the division of a nation. Touching them with remembering hands gives shape to and an opportunity for healing buried grief, both private and communal.

Early on that Sunday morning, there were already many flowers and notes placed tenderly against the wall. I paused to read one of the notes, which included a clipping from a small-town newspaper. The article carried a picture of a young man in a dress uniform who had died twenty-five years earlier. There was a poem next to the picture written by the young man's family as an observance of the anniversary:

We only lent him to you,
and he was taken away.
Now he lives on in our hearts,
a hero, but we still miss him.

The poem was propped against the panel where the young man's name carved into stone carried the sorrow of hearts of flesh. The freshness of the soldier's face, frozen in time at the age of twenty, made the horror of his death starkly obvious.

At the next panel, two women who had never met exchanged tips about making a rubbing of a name. One of the women tore a piece of paper out of her notebook and handed it to the other saying, "Do you have a pencil?" The woman answered that she did, and standing on her husband's knee, she tenderly rubbed the pencil over her brother's name. The woman who had provided the paper looked from a distance at the rubbing and said, "Good, it worked." Satisfied, she went on her way, the tactile exchange of materials and grief hanging quietly in the air, as the other woman carefully folded the paper with her brother's name and placed it inside her purse.

Near the center of the panels, a small group of people were gathered in a semicircle. Two men stood in front of the wall. One man, middle-aged, wore a jacket that designated him as a Vietnam veteran. The other man was older, dressed in a simple spring jacket and slightly bent as he stood next to the wall. In one hand he held a small azalea plant. In the other, he tightly held a piece of paper from which he read:

Our son was called upon to make the ultimate sacrifice for his country. We gather here today to put these flowers in front of his name and honor him for what he did. Son, we're proud of you, and we'll always love you.

When he finished reading, the father folded the paper in half and, lifting his glasses, rubbed his eyes with the back of his hands. He then stooped carefully and, as if the action caused him great pain, placed the bright pink azalea on the ground in front of the wall. He turned, lifted his right arm up over his head, and tenderly touched the name of his son. The other man touched the father's shoulder, and they walked away from the wall to join the rest of the family.

Waiting for him were three women, two of them middle-aged. Between them stood a stocky, elderly woman with tight gray curls and a handkerchief that her nervous fingers had twisted into knots. Pointing toward the azalea plant and the name on the wall, one of the younger women gently touched her mother's arm and said, "Maybe now you can talk about him, Mom." The mother shook her head up and down and walked quietly toward the engraved name of her son. The family stood around her in a semicircle as she touched her son's name. Tears spilled down their cheeks as, one-by-one, the whole family touched the name and stepped away from the wall. Their accents indicated that the family was not from the Washington area. They came on a pilgrimage that Sunday morning to break through walled-off pain that had made it impossible for a mother to speak of her son. In that moment, they had found expression for their grief and the possibility of rebirth. They hugged each other and stood by the wall for a long time.

A father and his young son walked by the family. The little boy, himself a potential soldier, said to his father, "It's really sad how all of these people died." Respectfully looking away from the family gathered in their grief, the father simply answered, "Yes, it is." There had been controversy over the design of the wall because it was thought by some to be too passive and not celebratory of the heroism of the war. As it stands, there are no arguments about the war, who was responsible for it, or what should or might have been done differently. In that place, there is a pause to simply say how sad it is that all of those people died and to pray for peace in the hearts of all who grieve its losses.

~❧~

Next to the wall is the recently dedicated Vietnam Women's Memorial. The sculpture of women tending the wounded was a major step forward in making visible the reality of women who suffered through the war and whose stories, like so many mothers' losses, had fallen into a silent abyss. The women in the sculpture look alive, their faces twisted in anguished concentration as they minister to the latest round of pain. Like the wall, the stones of the women's memorial fairly shout the memory of suffering. Bouquets of flowers at the base say that this, too, is a place of offering symbols that give permission to speak of memories too long silenced. I sat by the women's memorial for a few minutes, transfixed by what felt like the still-watchful eyes of those who tended war's wounds. The band at the Lincoln Memorial was playing the "Battle Hymn of the Republic." The music no longer felt like the triumph of spring but felt rather like a sad commentary on the historical continuity of violence, war, and pain.

The sun had stopped shining as I walked toward the train station. A powerful April wind stirred up dust in anticipation of rain that did not come right away. The dust made it hard to breath, even as the promise of rain held a cleansing power. When the rain finally came, it brought with it a great sense of relief, as if the sky itself was offering tears. People on the street commented that the force of the rain might harm the cherry blossoms. Those beautiful blossoms seemed less engaging to me after the visit to the Vietnam War Memorial. Or perhaps their beauty was made all the more compelling by the soulful agony and hopeful remembering of the monument. In either case, I appreciated the way in which the rain washed the air and diverted thoughts of tragedy, triumph, and rebirth. As I rode the train up the coast to New York, I recalled the family at the memorial, and somewhere in Delaware, I cried from a sadness much too deep to be mine alone.

The next time I was in Washington I was with my husband and sons. We were on a one-day trip that ended at the Smithsonian Museum of American History. A parade on Pennsylvania Avenue kept the museum from being very crowded that afternoon, which gave us a rare opportunity to wander the museum at our leisure and to linger at usually crowded exhibits. The lack of crowds allowed Dick and me each to visit in solitude the exhibit "Legacy: The Healing of the Nation." The legacy exhibit is a sample of objects that, like the poem and the azalea plant, have been left at the Vietnam War Memorial. Beginning with a Vietnam vet who threw his Purple Heart into the cement of the memorial's foundation, people have had a powerful need to touch the suffering and the memory by leaving flowers and symbolic objects at the wall. Like the family whose ritual I had witnessed, those who leave their offerings create a powerful sacramental connection between themselves and the world of sorrow created by the war, an expression that creates space for grief to breathe. Each night, the Parks Service gathers up the offerings and takes them to a warehouse where they are dated and catalogued. Everyone seems to understand that these objects are sacred and must not be destroyed, a respect symbolized in a policy that sealed letters left at the wall are to be saved but never opened. Even though the offerings are collected at the end of each day, grief knows no regular hours, and the wall is almost never without some tender object resting against it.

Gathered together in the legacy exhibit, the objects left by individuals became powerful symbols of a collective pain. Attendance that exceeded all expectation suggested that the exhibit touched a place of mourning within the national psyche. Knowing how large the crowds had been, it was strange to stand alone before the exhibit. The rituals I had witnessed at the wall never far from my consciousness, I slowly moved past the glass cases. A few of the objects in the exhibit had been found at the wall with notes addressing them to specific people. For the most part, though, the objects that appear at the memorial are mysterious and wordless in their origin and specific meanings. Yet, individually and collectively, they are testimony to the losses and grief that do not end by declarations and to relationships that do not end with death. The powerful symbols cast from the molds of ordinary objects touch a painful past and beckon forth prayers for peace.

There is a great variety in the offerings at the wall. People have quietly placed birthday cards and wedding pictures. Behind the glass were letters from veterans that described their healing process in gripping detail and, in the process, bade farewell to friends who had died too young. Someone left a fully decorated Christmas tree at the wall that stood silently in the exhibit, surrounded by army boots, wedding rings, photographs, and wreaths. Hundreds of the POW bracelets that were worn during the war have been left at the wall as signs of continuing memory. Nurses' caps, uniforms, ribbons, watches, and many, many flowers have carried the losses to the center of consciousness. And lest anyone forget that part of what was lost in Vietnam was the wonder and youth of a generation, there are toys resting poignantly among the boots and bracelets. One teddy bear had a note pinned to its chest by a mother who addressed the note to her dead son. The mother wrote that she bought a new bear to bring to the wall because she wanted to keep her son's original bear. She wrote that she carried in her heart the memory of how he had cuddled his bear through the night. I thought again of the mother at the wall who had been unable to speak of her son for twenty years, of her daughters' comfort, and of my own small sons holding their bears as they fall asleep.

Together, the symbols at the wall and the journeys they represent bridge the abyss between indescribable losses and the need to make meaning of the pain. The reality of people day after day bringing everyday objects to the polished, granite wall gives shape to a sense of grief beyond telling, which reaches for the heart of God to hold it. The very last item, indeed, the last word of the exhibit, caught me by surprise. It was a sign that had been hung on the wall in 1991. It said in bold, triumphant letters: "THIS TIME WE WON."

I stood before the sign for what felt like a very long time, the echoes of the "Battle Hymn of the Republic" in my mind. I was unaware that my husband and children had entered the exhibit until my four-year-old son grabbed my hand and said, "Mama, come quick! Did you see the lamb?" He pulled me away from the triumphant sign to the middle of the exhibit. High on a shelf was a stuffed baby lamb of the type commonly placed in babies' cribs. It sat there in the middle of hundreds of symbols of pain as if it were standing watch. It was the most haunting thing I have ever seen.

I could not look at it for long because Patrick was pulling on me, excited to show me something in another part of the museum. As he pulled me out of the Legacy Exhibit and into the urgency of his aliveness, I almost tripped over the artifact parked at the entrance of the exhibit. There rested an antiaircraft gun used in the Gulf War. That symbol of "the war we won" laid bare the grieving memory of the war we lost, and all of the innocence that died in its horror. The reminders of the Gulf War created a jarring dissonance.

What Patrick was so excited to show me was a femur from a Civil War amputation, resting in a glass case with the bullet still in it. He found the bone absolutely intriguing. I found it almost as haunting as the lamb because I knew that somewhere in the ground a body had turned to dust without a bone that some field surgeon had severed in a brutal procedure. Beyond the immediacy of its own history, the bone served as a startling reminder of how we arrange our national memory. The placement of guns and dry bones in such close proximity to the color and living grief of the Legacy Exhibit revealed something profound; it was more than merely an example of the Smithsonian's tendency — a frequent cause of complaint — to arrange objects as haphazardly as in an attic. From the powerful emotion of the Vietnam memorials and the legacy exhibit, the signs of triumph and strangely arranged bones spoke to a deeper pattern in the way we temper and arrange memory within the context of acceptable understandings. What would lay bare our grief is contained. As a nation, we do not do well with offering compassion toward our individual and collective memory of suffering. Instead, we often choose to repress it, rewrite it, or let its symbols be seen only within the parameters of other victories and different songs. If we can proclaim that "this time we won," the profound suffering of Vietnam becomes an aberration to be bracketed from consciousness.

The crowds at the memorial and the symbols they leave behind testify to the reality that we desperately need to make a connection with memory and pain. Those who leave their offerings at the wall act with courage that breaks the silence of suffering and challenges some of our most precious national images and the assumption of victory that they contain. The palpable pain in the symbols bridges the gap of losses and the need for life to renew itself. The offerings are, one-by-one, the blossoming promise of peace through consciousness. To stand before the symbols and witness their grief is to allow one's heart to engage in a profound conversion process. And that is never a comfortable, or triumphant, proposition.

Contemplation of the honest, raw memory of pain is consistent with the Gospel sayings: "Blest are you who mourn, for you shall be comforted," and "Do this in memory of me." When we honestly touch the memory for what it is, contemplating its pain and believing in the power of peace to break through when, finally, we can talk about it all, we have a profound opportunity to experience the comfort promised to those who mourn. We can then experience, in the remembering spirit of the Gospel, forgiveness as liberation from the domination of the past. That liberation is impossible if we continually rewrite the past in our hearts. When we cannot touch the memory, make symbols, and let them speak their power, we not only have contained the truth of our experience but have broken our connection to the merciful, remembering God. If we cannot allow the loss, the sin, and the grief to be unmitigated by a need to proclaim triumph, there is precious little experience of mercy.

Memories and symbols root us in our experience both as individuals and as a human community. Shortly after our trip to the Legacy Exhibit, I had a conversation with a man who had returned from the Killing Fields Memorial in Cambodia, a country whose legacy of war is millions of people dead and enough unexploded land mines to maim the next several generations. Built on the site of a Pol Pot regime massacre, the memorial is filled with skulls and bones that are naked evidence of the horror that happened there. Those bones are not a century removed from the processes that severed them, and their starkness holds no possibility for songs or signs of triumphant victory. The man discussed walking in that place with a sense that the ground itself remembered the agony of what had happened there, its dust not only clogging the lungs but covering his own body with the memory of the dead. He told me that he felt as if he could not wash the Killing Fields from his body; he had been covered with the memory of events so horrific that his only possible response was to pray. While he spoke, I thought of the isolated femur and a father holding an azalea plant. Without hope of triumph such memory will, of necessity, stir the soul and ask God to grant mercy to us who are made of dust.

In that place of terror, we must reach for forgiveness through a God who holds compassionate memory. Facing so powerful a longing to understand and be made whole, it is tempting to try to remake reality by changing its symbols, bracketing them, falling silent, or simply making it all disappear. Yet the paradox that the Vietnam Memorial's healing power proclaims is that the symbols and the remembering, if left just as they are, can engender conversion and renewal of life. It is, in fact, in the remembering process that a powerful new experience of God is born. What first appear to be God's powerlessness and abandonment in the cavern of that sorrow become the compassionate embodiment of life itself. This life of God, this earth, this Body of Christ remember what has happened here and invite us to speak the power of our truth. The conversion represented by the symbols and journeys of remembering reflects the marvel that through the woundedness and compassion of Jesus, God is forever one with the sacred, remembering dust of human suffering. And when the living waters wash us, there may indeed be blossoms that fall from the trees, yet we are, nonetheless, brought to a celebration of life shared by all hearts that risk the power of compassionate communion with experience and pain.

The compassion of Jesus remembers not only that "you were slaves in Egypt" but that God has been present from the beginning to hear the cries of those who suffer and to respond, not with triumphant proclamations, but with an ever-present love. The cries of those who suffer, and those who make symbols of their pain, are not received by a passive God. The truth of compassion reflected in the Beatitudes and the remembering cross opens the heart to make connections with others. That compassion is as palpable as the giving of paper so that another person can make a comforting impression of her brother's name. God hears the cries of the Killing Fields, the mothers who left plants and toys at a granite wall, the nurses who left flowers for their friends, and each of us who would run away and hide from the sight of a heart torn apart by war of any kind. God gives us courage to be with one another in that suffering, just as it is.

Memory, like an estuary, tends to be a muddy place. It is, however, still a place of birth where our experience is met by God's rising, remembering tide. Human sorrow is written in God's heart without qualification or a need for triumphant modifiers. In this fertile place, the full circle of sin and blessing is known, and sacraments are made of the ordinary objects that hold our loving memory. To live in a compassion that births forgiveness is to take those memories and their symbols and, like the thousands of people who have made journeys to the wall, bring the suffering to the center of consciousness where it can be held by God who sees the lamb and weeps.

Walking amid those symbols one knows that the wound is held in life's certain promise of rebirth. Each symbol holds the remembrance of the kind of human suffering and grief that has, throughout history, led us to cry to God for mercy. That cry leads to an experience of God's presence that, like the cherry blossoms, proclaims a triumph of peace no one would expect in the harshest days of winter. Celebrating the sacrament of our memory and its losses instead of bracketing it moves us deeply into the mystery of being the Body of Christ. For if we are that body, we carry the fullness and sadness of its memory as a sacred trust. And our holding it gently gives breath to the mercy of the final word bravely spoken: God's living tenderness healing the wounded heart.

CHAPTER SEVEN

Anemia

❧

Jesus turned around and saw her and said,
"Courage, daughter!
Your faith has restored you to health."

—MATTHEW 10:22

NOVEMBER had inexplicably decided to pause, giving us a warm day between dreary rains that kept us housebound. Feeling beckoned by the sunshine, I packed the diaper bag with crackers and extra juice, carried the stroller down from the second-floor apartment, returned upstairs to put baby Patrick in the Snugli, and, holding Michael's hand, walked back down the steps. Patrick fell asleep quickly, his head securely resting against my chest as I pushed his brother in the stroller. Michael was filled with the wonder and enthusiasm of a three-year-old suddenly released to play outside. Swinging his legs with excitement at being in the sunshine, he observed that it was nice to have summer again.

When we reached the playground, Michael bounded out of the stroller and headed toward the sandbox, where he met a little boy named Jeffrey. As they played together, Jeffrey's mother sat down on the bench across from me. More accurately, she collapsed with a sigh that suggested this pale woman was very weary. We were two mothers in a city park, enjoying unexpected warmth and trying to keep an eye on our children. We began to talk in short sentences about the weather, our children, and the experience of being tired. I uttered a sentence or two about having been up in the night with the baby; she told me that her husband was working long hours, so she never caught up on her work or her rest. Then she added, almost as an afterthought, "And I'm anemic." She went on to talk about her history of anemia, what brand of iron pills she took, and her doctor's prognosis that it would take a long time for the strength of her blood to be restored. At the time it did not strike me as unusual that a stranger was suddenly telling me about her menstrual cycle and its effect on her blood count. I, and most of the women I knew, were having babies. Our bodies were expanded space that could somehow be more freely talked about, as if consulting and delivery rooms, and the interesting lack of inhibition people feel about touching pregnant women, brought processes normally described in private places into the public domain.

A good number of women I knew had experienced anemia and its accompanying fatigue and breathlessness. A few of my friends became anemic because of an inordinate loss of blood during childbirth itself. For them the change was dramatic, instantly recognized, and treated. Most of us, however, had a different experience. Our anemia developed a few lost cells at a time, through the process of pregnancy, breast-feeding, and the heavy periods that reflect the changing hormones and healing of the womb after childbirth. We adjusted, often attributing our tiredness and dizziness to the demands of our lives as young mothers. Our anemia was generally discovered accidentally when something else caused our cells to be counted. One of my friends adjusted over time to anemia so severe that her doctor said that if her blood counts had become so low all at once, she would have been in shock. "And I thought," she told me, "that I just needed more exercise."

She was not alone in her assumption that her diminished energy came as a result of some action, or lack of action, on her part. Most women I knew, including myself, were not inclined to think that there was something objectively, measurably wrong with our bodies. We tried to exercise more or to borrow energy from coffee or to pretend that we felt fine while we were simply suffering the effects of having bled too much over too long a time. Once the cause of our exhaustion was identified, we became stronger with treatments that ranged from iron pills to corrective surgery to stem the flood of blood. Most treatments were as gradual in their restoration of energy as was the original blood loss. What came as a surprise when we grew stronger was that there was an alternative to our exhaustion. We had simply lost a vision of our own well-being, a loss that had been as insidious and destructive as our bleeding.

It has been a few years since I've had a conversation about anemia with a stranger. My children and those of my friends are older, making us less inclined to talk about reproductive processes with the immediacy that made descriptions of anemia so easy to share. Yet I daily experience a kind of exhaustion of the spirit that makes me think of anemia as representative of a woman's struggle to maintain a sense of strength and well-being in a world that bleeds away her energy drop by drop, rendering her breathless and voiceless. A good many of us have adjusted too well to an erosion of strength that disempowers us over time and fundamentally robs us of our vision of wholeness. Lacking a way of bringing our experience into the public domain, we are left to feel its consequences privately, and we lose our vision of alternatives.

This is an experience of anemia that comes not from the expansive carrying of life but from a constriction of the life force within us — the lost gifts, the talent undeveloped, the forbidden desires, the series of events that teach us to speak in the conditional voice and put our anger to sleep. It is the ordinariness of the bleeding — the expectation and understanding that it is a part of life to which one must continually adjust — that, in the end, makes anemia of the spirit so difficult to recognize and overcome. Yet it is part of the life experience of every woman I know.

I will never forget the woman who told me about her life-long sadness at not having been able to go to high school and college. She had a natural curiosity and gifts in many areas that gave her a great desire to study. It was, however, unheard of for any woman in that family, or geographic area, to study beyond the eighth grade. The woman talked about how sad she was to have had no opportunity to study, hastening to add, "But that's just the way things were." Perhaps the saddest part of the story was that when her daughters had an opportunity to go to college, she did not encourage them, saying rather that there was no point in a woman getting her hopes too high or expecting too much from life. The impossibility of developing and expressing her gifts destroyed the woman's passion and ability to envision a different future for herself or her daughters. She survived the anger and the sadness by narrowing her view of herself and of wholeness, her dreams slowly bleeding away.

Her story and its message about expectations were striking to me because, by external measurements, my world had many more possibilities for women than the one she described. I had a professional position that represented a conscious effort to integrate women into a male-dominated organization. I was the first woman appointed to several committees, frequently the only woman in the room and, as such, a symbol of progress. Like anyone in a minority position I was called on to be the bridge that carried the emotional content of the situation and, when necessary, was the first to forgive. I daily experienced that although there were no laws or written rules stating what was possible for me, there was constant sabotage and impositions of strength that had an effect as narrowing as forbidding a woman to study.

I experienced this narrowing most directly through an insidious dynamic that had me constantly questioning my own experience of reality. I was slowly worn down to a sadness that tempted me to accept disempowerment and lowered expectations as the price of peace. Like the woman who mistook severe anemia for a lack of exercise, I kept thinking that I was doing something wrong or misinterpreting events or simply lacking strength. I could not understand why so much of what was proclaimed as progress for women left me feeling breathless and tired.

My job put me in a position to do a fair amount of public speaking. Following one such presentation, a man in a position of authority approached me. I was nervous when I saw him because he had several times made unwitnessed and threatening sexual comments to me. That day he stood too close, looked me in the eye, and, smiling, said, "You did a wonderful job." It would have been a happy compliment to receive were it not for the fact that while he was saying it, he wrapped his hands around my upper arms and squeezed them so tightly that my eyes filled with tears. He then shook me, repeating through clenched teeth, "a great job." As he walked away, he hit me on the back. That he punctuated complimentary words with behavior that hurt me made the encounter all the more confusing.

Yet what was most disempowering was that I did not feel the fury that the situation called for. Rather, I was filled with self-reproach and the nagging question of whether I was misinterpreting actions that left their stinging imprints on my upper arms and back. I managed to convince myself that though I had never seen him grab a man by the arms and shake him, I had seen him hit them on the back. Furthermore, I told myself, he probably didn't even know that he had hurt me or made me more hesitant about speaking in public. I trusted too little my perception that hostility was being directed against me and that I was being threatened by an implicit communication of superior physical strength. The encounter itself leaked some of my life away; that I could not name it increased the loss.

I was more careful after that experience, and certainly I was more afraid of the man in question. The fact that the dynamic was not terribly out of the ordinary, and in one form or another repeated almost daily, led me to longer silences. Thus it was somewhat uncharacteristic when during a conflictual portion of a committee meeting at which I was the only woman, I strongly expressed a dissenting opinion. None of the people on the board commented about my position during the meeting itself, though there was enough shifting of bodies in chairs to indicate disagreement. At the coffee break, one of the men approached me and began a strange monologue about, of all things, the Spanish Inquisition. After describing confessions of faith exacted under pain of death and the most effective means of torture, the man said to me, with a perfectly straight face: "The real problem with the church is that we quit burning witches." I was stunned by his comment, and then to my horror, I did the expected, acceptable thing: I smiled. But behind the mask of sanctioned emotion, I clearly understood that this was no joke, and it scared me.

Later in the same coffee break, I overheard another man suggesting that I made my observations out of a position of trauma and oversensitivity. The next day, a male consultant, who hadn't been present the day before, reported to the committee and expressed, almost verbatim, the views that I had stated. In response to his presentation, the man who had diagnosed me as unreliable by virtue of trauma thanked the consultant for having the courage to say what the group did not want to hear. Not wanting to be discredited as "an angry woman," I failed to point out to the man the obvious disparity in response to what was essentially the same information. Somehow I had the feeling that it was pointless; he probably didn't even recognize that the consultant and I had said the same thing or that my trauma was someone else's courage. And furthermore, I was too tired to try to explain.

Perhaps the most painful and confusing part of the experience was that my presence on the board was heralded as a sign of progress and openness, and even as I was leaving the room feeling wounded, intimidated, and insulted, the men were congratulating themselves for having allowed me to be there. One of them went so far as to tell me how beautifully I fit in, an affirmation that was possible precisely because I was afraid to speak. But what most bled away my strength was the impossibility of expressing the impact of these events on me. I stayed silent out of my own fear and to protect the possibility of women having some point of entry into what had previously been a closed system. It was also true that the events at that particular meeting, and the relational patterns that supported them, were too embedded in everyone's consciousness, including my own, for me to unravel them. The most profound difficulty, however, was that the same socialization that teaches women to suppress the anger that naturally arises from mistreatment demands that we take care of the very people who inflict the worst injuries. Thus, even as I felt afraid, I smiled to avoid offending a man who was branding fear in my head by talking with admiration about the horrendous death of six million women burned as witches.

I have heard and witnessed a great many stories about oppression and appalling events that cause women to hemorrhage and go into shock. My own experience of oppression pales in comparison to the brutality inflicted upon the majority of women in the world. Yet what we clearly have in common is the truth that the most debilitating element in any abusive situation is the desolation of feeling cut off from the human community. My experience of disempowerment happened in a day-to-day context in which, all claims for progress notwithstanding, I was totally isolated. I could not bear witness to the impact of the experience, and I could not feel my own anger as a source of life. Anger in a woman that has no place to go becomes a wounded, bleeding womb that loses its strength to carry new life. The anger in me turned around and became self-reproach so quickly that I knew of its presence only as the breathless anemia that weakened my voice. Sometimes in the silence that was created by my isolation I thought about a woman I knew whose only form of self-expression was the way she cooked. The year she made grilled cheese sandwiches for Thanksgiving dinner, everyone assumed that she was angry about something. She said that the problem was she'd been too busy to buy a turkey. When people began to comment that I had become quieter, I answered that I had simply run out of things to say, and, on some level of my being, I believed that to be true.

Like the women whose anemia was discovered in the course of diagnosis of other problems, I encountered the real meaning of my silence when I began studies and found that mine was a common experience. Taking my own experience seriously gave me the ear to hear the stories of other women and to have compassion for their struggles. I learned that if I am to respond authentically to the suffering of other women, I must take my own slow bleeding seriously and envision a different way for all of us to be in the world. I came to understand that reaching out from the isolated space brings the individual experience of anemia into the public domain and creates energy to heal the common wound. And like physical anemia, exhaustion of the spirit takes time, and intervention, to heal.

A powerful model for this healing transformation is a woman whose life was saved by her determined faith in the face of circumstances that could have sent her away to die. The Gospel presents her story cryptically. She had been afflicted with a flow of blood for a dozen years. The pain she suffered in all of her previous treatments, her disappointment, and the isolation mandated by her ceaseless flow of blood formed the daily context of her story. Yet in spite of her exhaustion and all of the social conditioning that made her affliction the cause of shame and self-reproach, she did not lose her capacity either to believe she could become healthy or to literally reach for an alternative to her suffering. In her hesitant, yet purposeful, reaching for Jesus, the woman revealed the courage to acknowledge her suffering. Her faith allowed her to extend her hand from the periphery of the human community and to be received by the living God.

The woman's faith and Jesus' engagement with her transformed a cause of shame into the channel of God's healing grace. Jesus and the woman showed great courage in breaking the blood taboo; they both refused to accept the diminishment and constriction fostered by longstanding custom. That the gift of faith could be accessible to us and give women a power to reach from the shadows of isolation is a liberating idea. The faith shown by the woman in the Gospel holds the possibility that the very energy that bleeds from us can become a source of new life. That transformation requires an act of faith that expands our vision for ourselves beyond the exhaustion to which we are accustomed. Giving word to the flesh of our experience holds the power to transform smoldering embers that burn our own souls into the pillars of fire guiding us in the wilderness.

I have come to believe that the anger we feel is a call for life and, as such, is a sign of God's presence. Properly understood as energy for life, the anger can keep us from surrendering to circumstances against which we need to fight. It can also give us the vision to keep reaching out for the hem of God in the midst of our human community. The commonality of women's experience of disempowerment, isolation, constriction, and anger without word, even if arising from different and distinct life circumstances, forms a meeting place for an embodied experience of faith that restores us to health. To experience and express our anger, individually and collectively, is to refuse to accept our diminishment as the only possible reality. That faith is manifested in a determination to search out and address the causes of our exhaustion and breathlessness. It is an affirmation of God's life within us and a call to hold sacred our right to be whole and free of shame. The edge of the garment that heals is as near as the desire for health persisting in spite of all we have been told. Its hem gives us the faith to think and even to speak together of the strength to carry our own lives out to play in the sun.

CHAPTER EIGHT

Watercolors

For you darkness itself is not dark,
and night shines as the day.

—PSALM 139:12

S HE HAD, as a nurse, borne witness to a great deal of suffering, and she needed to open the circle of her pain by telling me some of her stories. I felt privileged to receive them. They were very sad tales that wound their way through betrayal, violence, abuse of innocent people, and death that seemed to be without meaning. At times it was hard to listen, and I prayed in silence for the hospitality of heart to hear of so much human woundedness. After she had been talking for some time, she began to tell me the story of a little girl that she knew during a year of service in Africa. The child was full of life and curiosity as she approached the age when the genitals of women are, through a socially mandated mutilation but civilly illegal act, turned into scar tissue. She unsuccessfully tried to convince the child's mother to reconsider; the mother told her that it was all necessary. The nurse knew that if the child escaped the passage at that moment, she would be mutilated at the time of her first delivery, when she would be equally powerless to resist.

The nurse was told by a neighbor that the woman who performed the procedure had come to the area, and then she noticed that all of the girls of a certain age were suddenly absent. A few days later, she was beckoned by the mother of the lively little girl to come and, as the mother said, "visit the wound." The purpose of the visit was not to offer medical assistance of any kind but to give witness as an adult woman to the child's passage. There was great trust implied in the invitation, yet the nurse felt hesitation because of the complexities of the wound and its meaning as an initiation.

When she visited the child, and her wound, the nurse was deeply saddened by the stillness of the previously active girl. She described the wound itself as "gruesome." After a time she paused and said to me, "I have seen people who were desperately ill or critically wounded express faith in God and truly believe it, while more and more, I would wonder where God has gone. That was a day when I wondered more than usual. The suffering of children always makes me wonder more than usual. But it was the inescapability of it all that bothered me the most." She did not stop with the story of the little girl but told story after story about suffering people on two continents and the mysterious way in which faith seems to flourish in the most trying of circumstances. And still, she wondered.

As sometimes happens when one is privileged to hear a lot of life stories, I felt in her words an echo of my own doubts and struggles. I was silent as she spoke, and sometimes in the midst of her powerful narrative, I grounded myself by watching the dust in the sunlight between us. After she left me, the distraction I experienced as I tried to distance myself from her stories and questions began to feel like a holy longing that tugged at my sleeve. The inescapability of the suffering, indeed. For some time I had been bumping into the truth that I was holding out against experiencing the limits of my images of God for fear that attention to their inadequacy would break what felt like a very fragile connection.

Like a change of season, the experience of God's absence was at first as subtle as the shifting angle of sunlight in my kitchen. If one is serious about the spiritual journey, there must sooner or later come an experience of limits wherein one knows that every image and idea about God is inadequate. At times, that experience of inadequacy makes God seem inaccessible, as though there is no way to approach so powerful a mystery. In the confrontation with suffering, there is also a failure of God as I wanted God to be, and in that failure comes a silence that is the emptiness left behind by false images. I know that the masters all agree that what first appears as the loss of faith is often God calling us to a deeper place of knowing; however, that whispering of the spirit has at times brought precious little comfort to the barren soul. Praying from this profound experience of silence and barrenness, I find it to be a turning point like the winter solstice — dark, cold, and difficult but nonetheless the beginning of a transition toward new life.

Following my conversation with the nurse, I found myself increasingly unable to find peace or comfort in prayer. Instead, when I went to the quiet places, I found agonizing images of a world seemingly gone mad without intervention from a loving God. What I was most aware of, particularly in my distraction, was my intense desire to make it all go away. As I entered the transitional darkness that began with my distraction, I repeatedly visited wounded moments when I had fought against the feeling that God abandoned the most vulnerable people in the world. There were more such moments within me than I first suspected, and I seemed drawn to visit them at a time when I felt neither courageous nor, as we used to say, in a state of grace. I was without confidence that God stood with me in the exploration. God, in fact, seemed curiously silent; it was as if everything that had served as a source of connection between myself and God suddenly became an impediment instead. At the same time, I experienced the paradoxical reality that the God for whom I had no words or name was waiting for me somewhere in the darkness.

I had been living for some time in the complexity of that reality when the Salvadoran military brutally murdered six Jesuit priests, their housekeeper, and her young daughter. It was a horrible crime in a nation that had suffered decades of violence. It shocked people in no small part because the military seemed to have no fear of international censure for killing priests or innocent women; it seemed to signal once again that the military felt licensed to kill. Several thousand people took to the streets of Washington to increase consciousness of the horrors in El Salvador and demand a suspension of U.S. aid to a government that murdered its own people. I stood with the crowd in Lafayette Park, the end point of the protest, and watched November light fade over the White House, feeling as though the darkness in the world was far more pervasive than the light. Speakers testified to the horrors they had experienced and witnessed in El Salvador, and the crowd grew more and more restless in the presence of those testimonies.

While the speakers were telling their stories, the Washington police came with horses and cars, holding clubs tightly in their hands. They formed a cordon around the park and announced that anyone attempting to cross Pennsylvania Avenue would be arrested. A line of protesters quickly formed along the curb, eye-to-eye with the police. There was a long pause in which no one moved. Then someone in the crowd began to scream insulting things at the police. A small group joined the yelling, accusing the police of being complicit with murder. The police moved in more tightly around the park. Their movement and the screaming added to the tension on the curb and increased the drama of the confrontation. A minority of people were making all the noise, and the sentiments that they expressed were far from the commitment to peace that was the purpose of the march. However, anyone who was in that section of the park was drawn into a growing spirit of hatred that made everyone vulnerable to the results of a confrontation with the police.

I stepped back a few feet from the curb with the realization that while I didn't particularly trust the police, I had no more confidence in the people standing immediately around me. We were all capable of reducing each other to the symbols or emblems that make violence possible. As I felt the growing tension, I discovered that I was experiencing both nervousness and a total failure of righteousness. In that moment, I hated the police, the people around me, the Salvadoran military, and, for good measure, most of Congress. I was humbled to discover the ease with which something that began as a witness for life and peace could so easily become a way of knowing my own capacity for hatred. I felt deeply impacted by evil, not as an abstraction, but as the capacity for pursuit of the highest good to become a source of experiencing and justifying wrongdoing. I realized that I could step off a curb into hatred and violence as easily as anyone else. Suddenly we were all under the same shadow of sin that could not be pushed back, projected, or denied.

Eventually those who were making the most noise quieted down, and a group of people — those who had dwelled long enough in their capacity for evil to be disciplined in their presence for peace — stepped off the curb and quietly offered themselves for arrest. The crowd in the park began to sing, bringing forth a more gentle spirit, even as the police and protesters encountered one another. As we sang, I thought about the wrenching truth that the particular murders we remembered in the streets that day were representative of thousands of deaths, not only in El Salvador, but throughout the world. Many of the dead were children. I thought about the darkness I had discovered in my own heart. The vengeance I wanted was but a glimpse of the human capacity for violence. Equally powerful within me was the desire to make it all go away and to live without consciousness of either life of death. I did not, in that moment, consider myself a murderer, but I did catch a glimpse of another dimension of my own humanity. I felt both witness to great sin and capable of great sin. In the experience of that paradox, I sensed that God was not as distant as I had imagined.

Until that afternoon, I had not understood why the Desert Fathers and Mothers wrote so much about sin and compunction as constantly present in the life of anyone who would seek to be holy. I had always hoped that if the world got holy enough, if I got holy enough, sin would disappear. That belief was my implicit understanding and the source of my images of the reign of God. Experiencing a standoff with the Washington police led me to know the limits of my own power to be a righteous presence for peace. And I understood that God seemed absent to me because I was afraid to see the darkness and believe that there could still be divine presence and mercy. It occurred to me that perhaps the reign of God is more profound, and more present, in the complexities of human life and suffering than I had dared to suspect. Perhaps it was that presence known in the midst of weakness and frailty that had inspired the songs of praise described to me by the nurse. What at first appeared as God's distance was simply the room I needed to discover the limitations of my own ego and understanding and to be embraced by the living God. I stood in that awareness like one entering an unexplored castle — I felt fear but also sensed a quality of hospitality and grace.

It was the middle of the night when I got home. The images of the day tossed me about as I tried to sleep. I had just dozed off when I was awakened by the familiar sound of Patrick with the croup. We had been through the croup a half-dozen times by then, so I was no longer surprised by the suddenness of its onset or scared by the sound of the cough. I stumbled into his room, picked him up, and carried him down to the bathroom. As the steam from the running shower turned our hair into ringlets, Patrick's breathing began to ease. He relaxed in my arms and fell asleep with confidence that I would hold him in the night. I did hold him, first in the bathroom and then in the rocking chair. I felt drawn in by his breathing, and I waited, keeping his lungs clear by holding him upright in the darkness. The morning light came too quickly and found me sleeping with Patrick still in my arms, his cough a distant memory and the shadows of Washington all the more powerful in my mind.

I have gradually come to understand those shadows as home. Breathing in an awareness of sin, the inescapability of suffering, and the reality that God is not the powerful magician I might seek makes it possible to be open to the surprises of grace. What I first perceived as the failure of my prayers, or the failure of God, was, in fact, the transformation of belief. When my distraction and restlessness became apparent to me in the context of listening to another person describe her experience of doubt, I wanted to resolve my distress as quickly as possible. It has taken time, several journeys into the darkness, and more than a few tender moments caring for my children for me to realize that resolution is often not the goal in spiritual life. Faith is as much a matter of standing patiently in the darkness as it is rejoicing in the light. It is, in fact, the essence of grace that God joins us in darkness and shadows, making them the place of consolation. I am contented to live there and be moved and changed by the experience of my own powerlessness.

Faith cannot always draw its images or inspiration from an object or an experience of God in direct view. Sometimes, like an Oriental watercolor, the essence of life is captured only in the contemplation and remembering. A new understanding and expression of faith are born of yielding to the mystery that God is so much greater than any one of my images. Faith truly is a gift, its essence often most keenly known when we feel far away from the source of life and, in fact, while standing in the shadow of sin and death. It is then that we find that God, who had seemed absent, is as much a part of us as the water that forms our cells and bonds color to paper. That mysterious essence of God holds us tenderly, that we might breathe freely through the experience of spiritual night — and find in it, peace.

CHAPTER NINE

Stiffness and Grace

*My being proclaims the greatness of the Lord;
my spirit finds joy in God my savior.*

—LUKE 1:46

THE PAIN crept up on me so insidiously that I have never been able to pinpoint exactly when it all started. What first caught my attention, I remember, was the fatigue. I not only wore out more quickly than I ever had, but at times I experienced sudden waves of exhaustion that felt like the life force was leaving me. I felt stiff when I awoke in the morning, and sometimes when I tried to stand up from a chair, I felt as if my bones had frozen in place. My hands ached, and I often lost my grip on things; simple tasks like opening jars became more and more difficult. I was very tired, and I felt as though I was dragging myself through life with a low-grade case of the flu.

Because of the creeping nature of the symptoms, I mostly ignored them or attributed my discomfort to stress. It never really occurred to me that something more serious than overexertion could be happening in my body because I considered illness an insult that simply would not be coming my way in the foreseeable future. I pushed through the symptoms for quite a while, going about my life as a wife, mother, administrator, and graduate student, a combination that in and of itself should have given me pause.

Shortly after my thirty-fifth birthday it dawned on me that I live on the edge of the forest in an area where Lyme disease is prevalent and that it might be wise to see a doctor. I thought that by going to the doctor, I could either eliminate the Lyme bacteria from my system or, failing that diagnosis, admit that I needed more sleep and get on with it. I described my symptoms rather glibly to the doctor, who responded by scribbling furiously in my chart and telling me that I did not have classic Lyme symptoms. He did not offer an alternative diagnosis. He would order some blood work, he said, and get back to me. I left his office thinking that his silence was good news and that I had known all along there was really nothing wrong with me that finishing graduate school wouldn't cure.

The next day as I was rushing between meetings at my office, my secretary handed me a message from the doctor's office. I was alarmed that he had called so quickly, since I knew from previous experience that doctors are not nearly so prompt about calling with normal test results. When I returned his call, the doctor told me that he would like to see me again that afternoon. As I went to my next meeting, I spared myself from worry by pushing the conversation with the doctor as far from consciousness as I had the symptoms themselves.

Later in the day, I learned from the doctor that the combination of my symptoms and the presence of the rheumatoid factor in my blood led to a diagnosis of a classic case of rheumatoid arthritis. He explained that rheumatoid arthritis is an auto-immune disorder: something triggers the immune system to turn against the body's own tissues, causing inflammation, pain, and joint destruction. It is a systemic illness that can affect the vital organs, and he told me that it needs to be treated seriously. I listened to him with the detachment of someone who was being overwhelmed, more fascinated by his description of joint construction than unnerved by the reality that he was telling me that I was a classic example of persons inflicted with a crippling disease.

The doctor told me that the course of the disease is difficult to predict and that medical intervention is extremely important in the early stages to prevent excessive joint damage. He talked to me about the importance of exercise, rest, and proper diet and prescribed a nonsteroidal anti-inflammatory drug that would help with the pain but not arrest the underlying disease process. Handing me the prescription, he said, "There's no reason for you to have an unnecessary amount of pain," a remark that caught me by surprise because it acknowledged something that I admitted only in consulting rooms, and then only under duress: the pain was real.

My response to the reality of the diagnosis was to set my jaw in a kind of determination that has characterized my approach to adversity. The words "chronic," "crippling," and "debilitating" did not yet have experiential meaning for me; I was in the beginning stages of even admitting the possibility of my illness. I seized on the doctor's comments about exercise, immediately making plans to return to swimming as a means of keeping in shape. I was determined to do everything in my power to manage the disease, and with that commitment firm in my mind, I took the first dose of the medication and returned to the demands of my busy life.

Had it been possible to "conquer" my arthritis through a combination of denial and sheer cussedness, I would have done it in those first months of my well-defined battle. My return to the swimming pool as a means of combating arthritis initially gave me a sense of mastery. I told myself that I was doing what I needed to do, and things would work out fine. I soon discovered, however, that I tired quickly in the pool and that I could not swim as fast as I had in the past. I learned that if I pushed too hard, my joints ached for hours after I left the pool; exercise-induced injury, my doctor called it. I needed to keep moving, keep swimming, but I needed to be slower and more deliberate about it, instructions that ran contrary to my character and expectation of life. In those first months after my diagnosis, I was particularly stubborn and cycled again and again through denial and exhaustion, unconvinced that force of will was not the solution to the illness.

I paid with throbbing pain for the mistake of pushing against symptoms that I should have greeted as messengers. Still I went about my life, trying as much as possible to compartmentalize the reality of my illness. Soon the days when I could convince myself I was healthy and in control became fewer and fewer. The pain began to represent a line of demarcation in my life between the time I felt healthy and truly in control and the time I knew that I had limits. Each attempt to deny or control my illness threw me into a confrontation with my silent and treasured beliefs about the terms of life. The pain and fatigue of arthritis forced me to reconsider my expectations and belief that illness, death, and limits are the domain of others, people to whom I can be present but whose ranks I surely need not join while still in my thirties.

I can recall late nights in college lounges when I sat with my friends and we sketched out a vision of our future and what we thought was possible for ourselves as women. We were the women born at the end of the boom, nurtured with traditional role models and expectations that settled deep within us and formed an unrecognized pattern for how we would be with our own children. At the same time, we were coming of age in a time of increased opportunities for women that gave us an expectation, indeed, an imperative, to make our mark in the world in a way that had been impossible for women of previous generations. We had expectations, both stated and unconscious, that it would be possible for us to have it all. It was not only possible — there was a certain urgency about forging our path in ways that responded to each and every expectation. When we stayed up late talking about our plans, it never occurred to any of us that all of this trailblazing might make us tired, or that the physical demands of motherhood might, at least temporarily, consume us, or that we projected ourselves as always possessing the borrowed energy of youth. We did not have an adequate understanding of the external obstacles we would have to face as women or that there was much in life we could not will away with our expectations of success. Many of us were embedded in conflicting models and dreams that were fed by a standard of professional and relational perfection. As we set about living out our dreams, what we most needed was to find the space and permission to bring together conflicting models and expectations in a synthesis or new voice. For a variety of reasons, however, most of us lacked that permission, and we wound up establishing our lives with an expectation of productivity that multiplied the worst of all worlds; now we simply had more challenges to conquer. We set in motion a way of being in the world that we thought promised fullness of life, too young to know that it was at the cost of humanness.

For me, there was a theological and spiritual underpinning to that perfectionistic drive, an underpinning perhaps best described in terms of the ancient debate about justification by faith or by good works. I came down clearly on the side of good works, both in my self-definition and, in a deeper way, in my understanding of what I thought God expected of me. I read life and the Gospel through a warped prism that made words of liberation appear to be imperatives to work harder. Somehow I missed all of the parts about rest, renewal, and grace. After I had spent time in Latin America, my spirituality was the container for the rawness of the suffering I had witnessed there, and it drove me to work harder, as if those efforts could be the amulet protecting me from limitation, suffering, death, or a sense of complicity in oppression. I felt a terrible sense of urgency after returning from Latin America; I was overcome by the sin of the world and its human consequences. In a very real way, the experience broke my heart. I brought to that sense of limitation the only antidote I knew: to work like crazy for a better world. That solution may have temporarily saved me the pain of recognizing my powerlessness in the face of overwhelming circumstances, but ultimately it contributed to my exhaustion. Judging myself against the standards of June Cleaver, Gloria Steinem, and Dorothy Day made for a cacophony of voices inside me that were demanding and relentless. I worked hard at the office, baked cookies late at night, considered myself responsible for righting the world's wrongs, and, too seldom, surrendered to the night and its dreams.

While playing to the standards of my times and conditioning may have kept me from facing the realities of limitations and death, it also deprived me of joy in living. I missed the subtleties of life that can only be appreciated at a slower speed. Creation was often a backdrop for my flurry, except of course for those moments when I was reminded by my superego that all of creation holds the presence of God and that I had better slow down and take note of that or I might miss the key to it all! The incursion of illness in my life, and the increasingly obvious fact that I could not beat the illness into submission, made me know in a most experiential way that my body had limits, that I could not have it all, and that, yes, even I would have to live with the ultimate insult of death. The pain delivering that truth to my awareness brought in its wake great frustration. There was so much that I wanted to do, so much I felt I had to do, that I could not yield to my experience of physical limitation. It was terribly difficult for me even to admit that the pain existed because I viewed it as a weakness and a failure. I continued to believe, on some unconscious level, that if I just "did it right" I could make the illness go away. I could not entertain the reality that I am a person and people get sick; that would have brought me to an embrace of the blessed limitations of humanness that I could not yet tolerate. Instead, I continued to draw from the well of my previous experience and believed that I could somehow get it all under control. What that meant on the day-to-day level was that for a long time I kept doing as much as I ever had — I simply did it with more pain.

One year after my initial diagnosis, the pain was moving into my larger joints, robbing me of sleep and increasing my fatigue. While some days I could still bring down the curtain of denial, most of the time I was going through the day as if my life force had a slow leak. Rather suddenly, I lost my appetite, which seemed to symbolize everything that the illness was doing to me; there was no passion or energy left in my body. I was subsisting, and most days I struggled just to do that. While it furthered my fatigue, the loss of appetite also caused me to become thinner than I had been in years. People innocently interpreted my weight loss as the by-product of self-control and told me that I looked wonderful. When pressed for the secret of my weight-loss success, I generally just said that it had happened all by itself, something I desperately wished was true and an explanation that spared both parties, especially me, the humbling truth. The weight loss that made me look wonderful was quite concrete evidence of a disease process that I didn't want to admit to and that seemed to be spiraling out of control.

My reluctance to admit what the illness was doing to me made it difficult for me to describe my symptoms to my doctor. When I finally succeeded in communicating the extent to which the pain, fatigue, and loss of appetite were increasing, my doctor concluded that we probably needed to move to the next line of chemical intervention. He referred me to a rheumatologist who walked into the examining room, took one look at my feet, and announced, "You've got a vicious case." The comments robbed me of the last stronghold of my denial and brought me to a new stage in the journey — I learned in ways both simple and profound that I *am* a person, and people get sick. And sometimes, in the process, we are reborn.

The doctor showed me pictures and models of joints and slowly explained the disease process to me. He told me that there was evidence of the disease all over my body, repeating my first doctor's observation that I was a classic clinical case. This time through, the words "chronic," "debilitating," and "crippling" had much more experiential meaning than when I had first heard them eighteen months earlier. The doctor told me, "You have a fire burning inside of you, and I am going to throw buckets of water on it." The water, he said, would take the form of powerful medications that could control the disease process and keep me from becoming crippled, which was inevitable if we did not treat the disease aggressively.

He had a concern, however, that the symptoms I presented could also indicate lupus, a potentially life-threatening illness. He wanted to rule that out as a diagnosis before he began treating me with the powerful medications intended for rheumatoid arthritis. He wrote a prescription for more potent anti-inflammatory drugs, ordered blood work, including the lupus test, and the next day left the country for three weeks without making any provisions for me to receive the test results. I was thrown into a terrible gray space where I took new drugs that made my stomach burn and waited to find out whether or not I had lupus. I was fairly successful in occupying myself, so that I wouldn't dwell on the possibility of having lupus. However, I had never in my life felt so physically wretched for such a long period of time, and in my most unguarded moments, it was not difficult for me to think that I could be dying or, at the very least, being eroded by the vicissitudes of my own immune system in irreversible ways. I was faced with the prospect of life's limitations with a kind of immediacy that was deeply unsettling, and I wondered if I was strong enough to allow whatever was happening in my body to be a place of conversion. In my frustration, I seriously doubted that I was, and I simply wanted back my previous sense of immortality.

It was Good Friday when I returned to the doctor. He walked into the room and said, "I've got good news. You have garden variety rheumatoid arthritis, which might make your life miserable, but, hell, it won't kill you." The lupus test was negative. Repeating the need to treat my disease aggressively, the doctor explained the drug therapy that would control the progression of my "garden variety" autoimmune disorder. The following Monday I would begin taking a low dose of methotrexate, a drug that was originally used in the 1950s as a chemotherapy agent. It was observed then that people who had both cancer and rheumatoid arthritis suffered less from their arthritis symptoms when undergoing treatment with methotrexate. Its toxicity, however, led to the drug's being abandoned as a chemotherapy agent. Methotrexate came back on the medical scene in the 1970s when organ transplants created the need to find ways to suppress the immune system. It was used in much lower doses than for chemotherapy and was taken only once a week to give the liver and kidneys time to heal between doses. It was again observed that patients with rheumatoid arthritis experienced an improvement in the disease — a discovery that coincided with increased evidence that rheumatoid arthritis is caused by a disorder in the immune system.

The doctor explained all of this to me, taking care to reassure me that there was no reason to be afraid of methotrexate because my dosage would be relatively low and the once-a-week admin-istration of it had been highly effective for reduction of toxicity. Nonetheless, I would need to have my blood monitored every four weeks for as long as I was on the drug. When I asked him how long that would be, he replied, "If it works, for the rest of your life." And then, having taken such care to reassure me of the drug's innocence, he told me to carefully prevent pregnancy because methotrexate would poison my eggs. As he gave me the prescription he said, "You'll be all right, you're calm," an obser-vation I have heard before from doctors. Translated that means I am self-contained in situations where a little hysteria would go a long way.

Given that in one twenty-minute consultation I had been told that I had a bad case of a crippling disease that required treat-ment for the rest of my life with a drug that, because of its toxicity, precluded the possibility of having more children, hys-teria would have been a gift. But I had been told too much all at once, and so what predominated in my consciousness was the wonderful news that I was going to live, albeit with limitations and great changes. I could not begin to express my feelings about what had transpired in the doctor's office or, more significantly, what was transpiring in my body. When faced all at once with pain, the knowledge of limitations, and at the same time being given back the incredible gift of life, I needed to ground myself in the moment and cherish its precious, living reality. Trusting common wisdom that the secret to surviving overwhelming mo-ments is to do something simple, I stopped and bought a Coke. I drank it slowly, and it proved to be surprisingly sacramental.

I went home and told my husband what the doctor had said. We hugged each other in the kitchen and decided to go out for an early dinner, both to spare the effort of cooking and, on a deeper level, to be quiet and grateful for the blessings that suddenly felt very apparent to both of us. There was a precious understanding between us that without knowing the fullness of what the struggle might be, we shared enough strength to live with the illness. The promise to cherish each other in sickness and health was being embodied more quickly than we had imagined, and yet there was, that night, a curious calm that was more than self-containment. It was the quiet truth of commitment to each other lived out in day-to-day realities as profound as changing energy and a lost sense of self and as simple as the tasks I could no longer perform. "We will live with this and adjust to it," Dick said, and I believed him.

After dinner, we took Michael and Patrick to a park on the Hudson River where they played with a kind of a joy that I received as pure breath of God. Like a person emerging from a dark cave, that evening I was crisply aware of everything around me, and I was profoundly grateful that I had eyes to see the world. I was overcome with gratitude for the lives of my two children, for the marriage from which they had come, and for the blessed knowledge that I would be there to watch my sons grow up. Their imaginations that night were particularly active — they played, built worlds around them, and called Dick and me from the park bench to join them in their imaginings. In that moment, the great gifts of life were mine to treasure, and treasure them I did. We watched the spring light fade into dusk, the children still at play, my heart still awakened to the simple marvel of being alive.

At nightfall we left the park and tucked the children in bed. I went shopping alone for the ingredients to make Easter dinner. I felt silly and happy and wonderfully alive in the grocery store, as if I had never before seen the colors of the vegetables or appreciated the funny ways people behave when choosing a check-out line. The act of putting food in the cart was a reaffirmation of life and resurrection more powerful than anything I could say in words. I knew that there was much adjustment ahead of me, and I was well aware of a certain anxiety hidden inside me, but, in that moment, I was gifted with a transforming experience of grace that made buying spinach an expression of the empty tomb. I was going to live, and each stiff step I took was affirmation of that gift. There would be time to deal with the pain, challenges, and limitations. Good Friday was my opportunity to receive strength and courage from the experience of living grace that suddenly, unexpectedly, was mine.

As things turned out, it was a moment of grace I would need to draw upon often. Easter Monday I took the first dose of methotrexate, and almost immediately it made me sick. I had been warned that the first few weeks on the drug could be difficult and that its control of the pain would not be experienced right away. I was unprepared, however, for the nausea and vertigo that the drug caused when at its peak concentration in the bloodstream. The doctor told me to be patient; I counted it as gift if I could work up the appetite to eat a poached egg. The pain persisted; the doctor said the dose was too low. He raised the dose and countered the nausea with a drug that tricked my brain and blocked its messages to my stomach. He drew my blood and said that I was not suffering from toxicity. I got thinner and received compliments from casual acquaintances about my weight and my hair, which suddenly changed colors and began to curl.

Several weeks and dosage adjustments later, methotrexate did significantly reduce my pain, but its side effects left me reeling. I considered it a major victory if I went for any entire day without feeling sick. Sometimes the effects of the medicine and the disease itself simply caved in on me, causing me to collapse in waves of exhaustion that I could not fight. It was then that all of my most grand designs and understandings, my good works and my good explanations, lost all of their meaning. Faith became as basic to me as breathing through the waves of nausea. Hope became attentiveness to the June roses as a source of strength; love became consciously choosing how I would act toward other people, in spite of how I felt. Courage became the act of living in the moment, trusting that some greater grace would carry me forward, and, mercifully, it did. Each time I passed through the waves of nausea or fatigue and accomplished something, regardless of how simple the act, I felt again to be celebrating the gifts of Easter.

I have often felt that what the illness and the treatment take away from me, they take in cruel, slow stages that I am forced to experience in absolutely every aspect of my life. Over time I have lost a number of simple pleasures, like tasting food and feeling hunger. Because of my desire to give my children a perfect world, I am pierced by the fear that they will have too many memories of a sick mother who had to say again and again, "I'm sorry; I can't do that; I'm just too tired." I always wanted to wrap my children in a world as soft as the receiving blankets in which I first held them, protecting them from pain and limitations. Instead, as must always happen with parents and children, I myself am the primary source for their learning that life is imperfect and unfair, and some things that we hate simply cannot be changed.

I have been thrown into a feeling of profound loss when, more than once, I have overheard my sons talking to each other about Daddy's being able to do more things than Mommy and about their concern over how much I need to sleep. When we go to the beach, I have to stay under the umbrella because the medication makes me vulnerable to the sun. That my need for such protection is real did not lessen the disappointment of my five-year-old son when I told him I couldn't help him build a castle on the edge of the water, as I had the year before. When he stomped off to build the castle himself, it was hard to see him through my tears.

As devastating as the side effects have been, I know that the methotrexate in fact controls my disease. Twice I have temporarily been taken off the medication in order to regulate the dosage. I experienced staggering pain and stiffness, which led me to understand "crippling" as a present, not a future, reality, one that is controlled with chemicals I find as difficult as the illness itself. During one of the disease flare-ups induced by a lack of medication, my doctor gave me frank advice about accepting the viciousness of the illness and making the compromises that are necessary to control it. The compromise requires me to choose the side effects of the medication over the pain and stiffness of the disease, which the doctor said is a good trade-off. While he was right, there are moments when all that I want is the normalcy of feeling genuinely, completely hungry.

That desire only serves to remind me of all the deeper compromises required in my life. I am called to make peace with the terms of limitation, not as an abstraction but as a hunger for wholeness that had no time to get lost in the drive for perfection. In my exhaustion, I have begun to pay more heed to what matters most to me in life because my body has no reserves from which to serve the gods of perfection. I do what I can do, and in truth, I find the compromises very difficult to bear. When it became painfully obvious that I needed the methotrexate to control the pain, I overcame my fear and a generalized anger that any of this was necessary and learned to inject myself with the methotrexate.

While not eliminating the side effects, taking the medication by injection lessens them. Each week I draw a small amount of yellow liquid from a vial that reads "CAUTION: SEVERE TOXICITY CAN DEVELOP FROM THIS DRUG," and, taking a deep breath, I stick the needle in my hip. I know that within a half-hour I will enter a kind of valley of death that shifts my focus from any abstract future thoughts or perfectionist leanings to the immediacy of surviving the first wave of vertigo. I truly don't get as sick as when I took the drug orally, but I am far from strong during the first seventy-two hours after my injection. I eat a lot of graham crackers those days, feel very vulnerable, and depend on the wisdom and competence of others. I am in those hours incapable of summoning the energy to do anything but live through the moment. My hips and arms have circles of tiny scars from the injections and the blood tests. When I experience all of those punctures, the veil between life and death feels very thin, and I am very tired.

And I find myself drawn to pray with, and for, all people in their suffering. When the effects of the medication or the disease are most merciless, I pray from exhaustion that leads me to collapse into the palpable care of God. I am mysteriously drawn to attend Mass and receive Communion, which gives me a wordless sense of being grounded in a story of suffering and resurrection larger than my own limited life. In that silent embrace, I understand grace as a reality much more powerful than my limited ability to work.

Methotrexate reduces the pain and slows the process, but it does not cure the illness. The disease has recently spread into the few joints that previously were spared, and my doctor has raised the likelihood of future surgery to correct deformities that are occurring in my fingers, in spite of all of the drug intervention. The circulation to my extremities has been compromised, so I now take a drug to address that problem. When I go to the pharmacy to refill my prescriptions, I feel angry at my dependence on drugs and medical insurance, and I resent that I must learn so much about feeling life's limits when I still have so many dreams. I hate the fact that I cannot depend on my body to be strong at a particular moment, a reality that has left me dragging through some rather important business meetings, struggling to stay in the conversation when energy was draining out of me. Like Jacob, I wrestle furiously with God over the fact that I cannot depend on the power of my own will. My wounded body is a constant reminder of the struggle to come to terms with who I really am. And who I really am is a human being who is as noble and as nasty as anyone else, a notion that comes to me as something of a relief. Not having the energy to try to save my own soul, I am learning that allowing myself to be human is an invitation to experience God's redemptive presence.

The illness undermines my confidence in subtle and not so subtle ways. I have greater awareness of the vulnerability of my opinions and perspectives, and I am less inclined to believe my own proclamations of truth. Frankly, I miss the certitude. But by far the most undermining element to deal with is never knowing when my energy will fail me or when I will be overtaken by pain and fatigue. There are predictable moments, such as right after I take the methotrexate, but I am just as often caught by surprise, which can be frightening and very frustrating.

There are, however, frequent moments of grace, occurring even in the midst of the moments of devastation. One such incident happened a few weeks before Christmas. I was riding the Number 1 subway train in New York City when I was suddenly overtaken by a wave of exhaustion and pain so powerful that I could barely move. Because it was not a day when I expected drug side effects, I suspected it was the disease process cycling through my body, which I knew meant the symptoms would eventually pass. I also knew that I needed to get home and rest. It was a powerful and frightening experience, particularly because the underworld, nightmarish qualities of the subway increased my sense of disorientation. When I worked up enough energy to step out of the train, I was captivated by the music reverberating off the tunnel. Someone was playing "Silent Night" on the violin. I walked toward the music, knowing that it would lead me to the entrance of the subway station.

I moved slowly but confidently, people rushing around me with the determined gait of those who, like myself in other moments, have no time to walk behind a person whose body or spirit is wounded. The music did, in fact, lead me toward home, where I rested, and by afternoon felt much stronger. The power of that experience was that for some time music has been a living metaphor for grace in my life. That day, walking toward the music gave me the means of negotiating my way through one of the more frightening experiences that comes with this illness.

I am described medically as suffering from severe rheumatoid arthritis that is "well controlled" with methotrexate and other medications. I know, however, that control can never be mine in the way that it was before a few years of illness made control a locus for my losses. I smacked right into my expectations of good works and the drive toward perfection, coming up sick and craving relief. I wanted to blaze a trail and change the world; instead I find myself rejoicing when I can open a jar for my son or slowly swim in waters that help me resist the pain. Rheumatoid arthritis indeed makes me miserable at times, a misery that springs as much from the prematurity of my encounter with limitations as it does from the physical effects of the disease itself. When it is at its worst, the illness makes each moment piercingly sharp and intense. Yet it is harder to grasp individual moments in retrospect because the pain and fatigue blur them together. That loss of capacity for memory is a source of deep pain because it symbolizes all of the losses of ordering and understanding. As a whole, the chronic presence of pain absorbs my life into a different pattern of remembering. I am constantly called to know that I am a human being, that I am ill, and that if I fail to acknowledge that truth, I will have even more pain than I do when I embrace it. There are many days when I am struck with fevers that cycle through my body, blur my senses, and leave me exhausted. The fevers remind me that while the fire that burns inside me has, on one level, been contained with chemicals, it is still present and constantly demanding attention. On a deeper level, this fire is groomed to become the kiln of a new creation. There is a personal transformation underway because of my illness. I cannot have it all, and in that acknowledgment lies salvation.

The most powerful thing this disease has done has been to call me to an attentiveness that births gratitude and joy in living. I am drawn to notice and love the world I once set out to conquer. There is a great joy in simply accepting the limitations and the gifts of being human. Surprisingly, those attitudes spring forth in me during moments of great pain and the experience of caving in to my exhaustion. It is then that I lack the ability, or the defenses, to remake life in my own images, and so I know myself as a child of God, needing love, needing care, and clothed in the blessing of divine presence I cannot control. For me to pause and notice the pattern of rain on the windows, the wonder of my children's view of the world, or all of the small ways my husband and I live our common life, feels like a very deep treasure. When I am blessed with clear, pain-free space, I am less and less inclined to fill it with activity that denies my disease and more drawn to cherish it as a source of renewal. I am learning to pray in a way that is a surrender to the grace-filled music, finding that the void of my losses can be a wilderness space where God whispers words of love. But this is a chronic illness, and I have cycled through peace and despair enough times to know that I will never neatly resolve the disease process or its emotional and spiritual meaning. Rather, I am called to live with its truths and allow myself to be reborn in the power of its limitations, a process that includes anger, frustration, and the very deep breath I must take each Wednesday morning before I inject myself with methotrexate.

All that I cannot do and conquer is teaching me that I greatly underestimated myself and other people when perfection drove me. I find that I am capable of much more than activity. Though I regularly pass through that valley that holds pain, fatigue, and weakness, I am much more alive than I was before I developed an illness. The irony of my experience is that what brought life and abundance to me was not my hectic pursuit of them but an illness that continually forces me to stop, be attentive, and receive the love of people around me. That love expresses itself in ways that are amazingly concrete: my friends help me with the children; Dick orders me little gifts and tools from catalogs that help me with the challenges of daily living. I am learning to ask for help, to respond honestly when people ask me how I am, and to tend to the simple things of life.

Unable to muster the energy to try to have it all, I receive the grace to cherish life as it is, imperfect and incomplete. Having been forced to see that I have less time and strength to work with than I thought, I am learning to find the horizon of meaning that guides me through the difficulties of the life I have. Ultimately we must all forgive God and ourselves for the reality that life betrays our youthful confidence and expectations. What is left behind when we have made the compromises, bowed to the truths of death and limitation, and discovered imperfection is an experience of the essence of life.

And that essence I must name as God — specifically, God functioning as the cloth that holds and unites the pieces of the story of my life, its sorrows, its joys, its pains, its misguided impulses, and its truth, in a way that warms me and, indeed, restores my life force in the midst of fatigue. I have less power than I thought, but when I surrender to the music, I have more strength than I had ever imagined. I surely would not have planned the pattern of my life to be drawn together by the unexpected threads of pain and limitations, nor would I have anticipated that the experience of a chronic illness would give me a renewed capacity for joy. But such is the mystery, and such is the experience of life that, for whatever reason, I am drawn to cherish. God meets me in the pain and invites me to make my life part of the common cloth, bound and stitched by the Spirit of one who lives among us. I find that presence comforting in simple and profound ways.

On days when my fingers are sore, it is hard to think of myself as stitching a wholeness of being. It is then that I am drawn to embrace the most profound lesson of them all: like everyone else, I am given this one life, with its limits and its capacity for dreaming. To live it well, I must surrender to the powerful presence of grace and receive its glory in my eroding bones. That means I must love and be loved in the ordinary events of the day. Feeling both broken and whole, I must let the scars of my punctures remind me that what matters is the relationship woven between people as we bring our scraps of life to each other, not the perfection of a design I would draw in advance, or in place of, living.

Several weeks ago my son Patrick said to me, "I'll bet if you had a magic lamp you would wish you weren't sick." Cherishing his tender hopes for my health, I asked myself if I would wish away the illness. And my truthful first impulse is that I would wish it away with death-defying speed. But since I have no magic lamp, and since defying death is no longer part of my illusion, I have to make a different choice. That choice is to let myself be remade in the experience of illness and believe in the sanctity of the journey of life itself. I celebrate that sanctity in an embodied truth that leads me to buy spinach and quilt life's mysteries in front of an empty tomb. When all is said and done, I offer thanks that in the midst of pain I have been given the great gift of life, not as I planned it to be, but better, infinitely better, because my limitations are stitching my life to the backing of the living God. I, who wanted to conquer and change the world, instead find myself connected in pain and powerlessness to sources of life much deeper than my own ego and much more enduring than my own ability to order reality. Such is the grace in my stiffness and pain, a simple joy in being alive, a music that leads me home. And such is the powerful blessing of the God who truly, and simply, is love.

EPILOGUE

Joy

❧

Go out in joy, return in peace; . . .
the thornbush has become a cypress tree.

—Isaiah 55:12, 13

I CALL IT the anguish tree. It is short with a dark trunk and expansive branches like a fruit tree. The relationship of the trunk to the branches makes the tree look remarkably human; the trunk has at midpoint an indentation that looks like a belly button, and it leans backward as if just out of sight there is a head that cries in pain. The branches are a multitude of arms reaching out of the twisted center toward the sky like a prayer. I first became aware of the tree during a long, wet winter when the ice on the branches made it look desolate and froze all memories of spring. When March turned solid ground to mud, the tree stood very still and wept the season's moisture through its bark.

As the changing sky of April yielded to May, the anguish tree blossomed and took me completely by surprise. The twisted trunk was less desolate when surrounded by pink flowers clinging to the very branches that had pierced the sky with their barrenness. The flowers lasted for a long time, each day sharpening their color and beauty. The first breezes of summer rustled through strong, green leaves on the tree, the outreached branches dancing with a delicacy not afforded them in winter winds.

The tree could bloom because, through the storms, it held the genetic memory of the life that comes again each spring; to celebrate life from death is its nature. The blooming of the anguish tree did not erase the memory of winter; it brought it to completion. So it is with the human capacity for joy. It comes not in the absence of limitations or brutal storms but as completion of a cycle of life imprinted in our souls that keeps us reaching outward in a celebration of God's presence. Joy is the blessing of the journey lived with integrity, the small acts and the great heroism that together make the suffering of one life reach for a broader sky that holds its meaning. Joy comes from the Spirit of God within us drawing us to sink our roots deep and experience a transformation through suffering and limitations. From such roots, the blossoms grow and renew our hearts.

When in quiet moments I count the blessings of my life, I know that what I most treasure is the reality that, over and over, I have seen the anguish tree bloom. In that capacity for transformation God's face is revealed in our day and time, generally where I least expect it, and always filled with gracious compassion. I wrap that joyous presence around my soul like a comforter made from scraps of life that God has held holy through the seasons. For the comforter, for the beauty of the anguish tree, for the power of the wilderness that teaches me to make a quilt, I offer thanks.

OF RELATED INTEREST

Margaret D. Minis
I DON'T MIND SUFFERING
AS LONG AS IT DOESN'T HURT

Margaret Minis has written a wry but comforting reflection on
"ordinary" life lived in the care of God for all those who have
ever had their life plans edited by a Higher Power.

0-8245-1438-6; $10.95

Paula D'Arcy
GIFT OF THE RED BIRD
A Spiritual Encounter

The heart's deep yearning for God, and God's answer, are vividly
described in the story of Paul D'Arcy's vision quest, a three-day
wilderness experience that follows years of grief recovery
after the terrible deaths of her husband and baby.

0-8245-1590-0; $14.95

*At your bookstore or, to order directly from the publisher, please send check or
money order (including $3.00 shipping for the first book and $1.00
for each additional book) to:*

THE CROSSROAD PUBLISHING COMPANY
370 LEXINGTON AVENUE, NEW YORK, NY 10017

We hope you enjoyed The Comforter. *Thank you for reading it.*

crossroad